ROAD WORTHY

JAMES W. ZIEGLER, M.D.

This book is written primarily for those mentioned within its covers, most of whom are (or have been) heroes in my life.

Special thanks to three people: First, thank you Dave Slone for your encouragement, assistance, and steadfast support. I consider you my co-author in this endeavor and a co-pilot in life. Second, thank you Ellen Birkman, sister and teacher extraordinaire, for the countless hours you spent guiding me through the writing process. Third, thank you Marlene Birkman for your extensive copy editing. I could not have written this book without the three of you. I consider its completion a team effort.

Also (in no particular order), I express my gratitude to Lisa Burditt, Kate Ziegler, Mike Denci, Gene Haltenhof, David Ashley, Heather Chapman, Milane LaRoy, Deb Adams, Jeff Redinger, Pete Pullen, Ross Hudson, Sara Ford, Evelyn Ziegler, Roger Bergh, Edie Engstrom, Al Beal, Jon McPhillips, Stuart Horowitz, Rich Pearce, and Matt Belisle for your input and constructive criticism. I especially thank my wife, Joy, for reviewing this manuscript several times and helping me mold it into its final form.

This book is dedicated to the memories of my father, my brother-in-law, an honorable Civil War veteran, and eleven young guys who died in the jungle of Vietnam the morning of September 20, 1970. The stories told within are their stories. My sincere hope is that these individuals will not be forgotten; that their legacies will live on through me, others they have touched, and you, the readers.

Finally, "Yes, Jimmy, I am ready!"

TABLE OF CONTENTS

Part 2

FOREWORD

When I was little and couldn't fall asleep, my dad used to lay in bed with me and tell me stories until I drifted off. He told me about growing up in Ohio and then Florida, about heading off to college and then medical school, about his travels and countless basketball games. We called the times described in those stories *"the lost years"* because they detailed the life he lived before he became the person I knew: a dad, a husband, a doctor, a friend, and a neighbor. I often wondered if my dad made these stories up, because at that time it was impossible for me to imagine that my parents had done anything cool or noteworthy before they became *my parents*—before they did things like lay in bed with me before I fell asleep. It was through these stories that I learned that before my dad was everything I knew him to be, he was a son, a brother, a basketball star, a student.

I always assumed that the only glimpse I'd ever get into *the lost years* was what I remembered from those bedtime tales and the select few stories that had become well-rehearsed family lore (like the fact that my dad only got a grade lower than an A in one college course because he "sliced his hand open" before the final, which seemed to come up every time our own college GPAs were reported). But then my dad told me he was writing a book. It seemed fitting that he would put pen to paper, because he's always been a storyteller to me.

We all know that we are a composite of the people who have preceded us—the family members and ancestors, and the influences that have pulled their lives in one direction or another. But

i

somewhere along the way, I think we often forget. We forget that we are marching along a road that bears the footprints of those who have come before us; we think we are forging our own paths in the world, going our own ways, making up our own rules. We may not follow others' footprints exactly—we may even deviate entirely—but we are still impacted by the crisscrossing paths and intersections and bridges and U-turns of history.

My grandfather was someone who never forgot this. When he picked up an old mallet in a thrift shop, one that most people would have cast aside, he realized he was holding a piece of the road of someone who had traveled before him. As an Army veteran, my grandfather immediately felt connected to whatever path had led the mallet's maker to Andersonville, Georgia, a notorious Civil War prison camp. And nearly thirty years after discovering the mallet, my grandfather diligently researched, planned, and then retraced that soldier's footsteps. A path long worn away by time was re-painted by my grandfather's efforts. A forgotten Civil War soldier was brought back to life.

In a similar way, this book was like a road map for me, because it gave me a chance to learn more about the paths taken by my dad and his dad before him. It also made me realize how often my own path actually veered onto theirs—followed along it for a little while and sometimes for a long while—without me realizing it. When I boarded an airplane to spend a year living in Thailand, a country I knew next to nothing about, I thought I was making a choice that was completely novel for anyone in my family. But this book clarified that many years before I took that flight, my grandfather boarded a troop ship to Japan, similarly bound to a completely unfamiliar place. The circumstances were entirely different, but I was retracing a path he had laid out for me.

Living in Thailand was exhilarating and nerve-wracking, fulfilling and lonely. I missed a lot over the course of my year there, from holidays to my sister's high school graduation. One of the things that was the hardest to miss was the bike trip my Dad was planning to embark on with—and in honor of—Dave Slone. For as long as I can remember, Dave and his wife Stephanie have been a part of our family. In addition, I had fallen in love with biking while in college in Vermont, so this was the type of opportunity I would have leapt at if I were stateside. Living so far away from home taught me to be creative in finding ways to feel close to my family and friends. So I decided to memorialize Dave's time as a solider in Vietnam and contribute to the bike trip from afar. I had the entire month of April 2016 to travel around Southeast Asia, and I set aside a week of that time for a solo trip to Vietnam. I obtained a few details from Dave about his time there and planned my trip around retracing some of his steps through the country.

I started in the south, in Ho Chi Minh City. Like my dad will describe in the second part of this book, I too knew very little about the Vietnam War, so I decided to make a trip to the War Remnants Museum. The current name reflects the improvement in diplomatic relations between Vietnam and the United States. Prior to 1995, the museum was named "Exhibition House for Crimes of War and Aggression." I found it important to remember that, as in any conflict, there were many different sides involved in this war, and this museum offered a different perspective of the conflict from the little I had previously learned in school. As I wandered through a room of photos displaying the effects of the chemical Agent Orange on Vietnamese civilians, I thought of Dave and the American soldiers he fought alongside, and all those from both countries forever affected by the international conflict into which they were thrown.

From Ho Chi Minh I flew to the seaside town of Da Nang, where Dave told me he had spent time in a military hospital. I wandered through Hoi An, a former trading port turned beautiful canal city, famous for its Japanese bridges and skilled tailors. Then—and this is the part of the story that I skated over when I told my parents exact details of what I would be doing in Vietnam—I met up with a tour guide named Fook, who had a rickety motorbike, some bungee cords, and two helmets. I secured my belongings, settled onto the back of his bike, taught Fook the phrase, "let's hit the road!" and we were off on a four-day motorbike tour heading north.

The main reason I wanted to do a motorbike tour was that it would take me right through the demilitarized zone, where Dave's helicopter had been shot down and his teammates and other soldiers had lost their lives. Fook and I wandered through the remnants of buildings bombed during the war and sped past breathtaking expanses of farmland and waterways. At one point, Fook asked me if I would like to stray from our route to spend the night with his family in his village. I immediately said yes. Fook's family was warm and inviting and cooked me one of the best meals I've ever eaten. With Fook translating, we discussed our lives and homes, and, eventually, the war. Fook's mom told me that she was a young girl during the peak of the war. Despite the devastation she witnessed, the thing that she most clearly remembered was American soldiers bringing candy and sweets to the children in her village. She said that now all she wants is peace, that she harbors no ill will towards the United States, and that she hopes many other Americans will travel to Vietnam to make new friends and experience the culture. In that moment, somewhere in the vicinity of where Dave's helicopter was tragically shot down years before and where Fook's family lost friends and loved ones, I saw that where governments and militaries fail, the human spirit can prevail. And although we forgive, we can never forget.

That thought stayed with me through September, when my dad, Dave, Steph, and Coleman left on their bike trip. I closely followed my dad's daily Facebook updates and Facetimed him as he biked. I again found myself wishing I could be there with my family and neighbors. I tried to find my own ways of getting involved. Recognizing the traction that my dad's Facebook posts were getting made me think that this was a story more people needed to hear, so I decided to contact local newspapers in Rhode Island to see if any would be interested in featuring a story about the bike ride. I had to explain over email to reporters asking if we could talk on the phone, that I was, in fact, in Thailand; that they should get in touch with my dad if they wanted to know more. I thought that the bike ride would make a nice human-interest piece, so I was shocked when, a few weeks after the trip ended, my dad sent me a picture of the *front page* of the Providence Journal bearing the headline "Riding with Honor."

Again, I thought that would be it. Those who happened to pick up a copy of the Providence Journal on September 21, 2016 would get to read an incredible story, but still one that would eventually be forgotten. And that is precisely why I am so glad that my dad decided to write this book, and so grateful he asked me to be a part of it. From *the lost years* to the lost souls, these are stories that deserve and need to be told. I love them because they are relevant and they are my dad's. I am also especially happy that my dorky, story-telling father can now touch others with his words, reflections, and wisdom.

Meg Ziegler, November 2020

INTRODUCTION
Three Signs

December 31, 2016

They say things come in threes. It certainly seems that way in my profession as a pediatric cardiologist. If I encounter two rare and bizarre cases, in short order I inevitably see a third. So it was with the impetus to write this book. I received what I interpreted as three "signs."

First, I was abruptly awakened out of a deep sleep by a voice that whispered, "Dave's survival in Vietnam was a miracle." I sat up in bed and looked out the window, down the hill at the moonlight shimmering off the bay. Did the voice in my head just tell me that my friend Dave's survival defied the laws of physics? That it was other-worldly? I had never been so intimately involved with a case of divine intervention before, but that was clearly the implication.

A few days later, I was driving home from work pondering the revelation that had jolted me out of a sound sleep a few nights previously. Deep within, I sensed a force gently urging me, but I felt confused. Why was Dave's amazing survival now at the forefront of my mind? What was I supposed to do? I looked at the sky above the road in front of me and half-heartedly asked God to give me a sign, to guide me. Now, I must admit, I have done this several times before and I've never received any overt signs. I have always interpreted that as God telling me He's got more important things to do; that I needed to figure things out myself. That particular winter evening, as I drove east toward Narragansett Bay, a golden-orange meteor appeared directly in front of me. With a long bright tail, it soared across the sky south to north, as if in slow motion, and then disappeared over the horizon. I smiled to myself and wondered if I had just witnessed what seemed to be another sign. If so, what did it mean? What was the message?

The third sign? On New Year's Eve, I decided to go running in a quaint little coastal village just north of my home. I have a three-mile loop there that snakes past the curbside federalist buildings that compose the core of the town. I have run the route hundreds of times, often with one of my daughters.

I parked in the middle of town, got out, and stretched on the sidewalk. It was a beautiful winter evening, cold but not frigid, with the sun below the horizon and darkness settling. It was completely still—very quiet and peaceful. I started jogging at a slow pace. As I warmed up my speed increased, and I began to breathe harder and sweat. My mind wandered. Halfway into my run, it was pitch-black, with only dimly lit, crooked streetlights and occasional passing cars illuminating my path. I knew every crack in the cement on this run, so I didn't need to see clearly.

As I rounded a corner into the last leg of the run, I contemplated the miracle of Dave's survival and the significance of the shooting star. Ahead of me, I saw a segment of uneven sidewalk with large branches from three ancient oak trees haphazardly spreading upward. I approached the first tree at a good pace. When I was within two strides of passing under its outstretched arms, a booming crack split the silence. A huge dead limb, unprovoked by anything apparent to me, crashed onto the sidewalk. Had I been two steps ahead, it would have crushed me.

I came to an abrupt halt and uneasily looked down at the rotted branch, its parts now scattered around me. I shuddered with the uncomfortable feeling that something (or someone) was urging me on, yet again. "Do it, before it's too late!" I recovered from the adrenaline rush of my near-death experience and completed my run.

Road Worthy

As I drove home, I thought of Dave. My brain was then flooded with other people's faces—my dad, my brother-in-law Arlan, friends, teammates, family members. They seemed to stream into my consciousness and dangle there as if held together by an invisible thread. I think the pleading inner voice I'd been hearing for the past several days was telling me I needed to bring these people together; to tell their stories.

When I got home, I jumped out of the car. I ran into the house and found my laptop on the window seat in our master bedroom. Right next to it was a plastic box that was latched. I had examined its contents earlier that day (as I randomly do every three or four weeks, usually for reasons unclear). I had forgotten to return the box to its usual storage place. I reached over and grabbed the small container and opened it. I looked at the wooden object inside. I gingerly picked it up. I realized the inanimate object I was staring at was the starting point...the connection. It and me. I grabbed my laptop and started typing.

PROLOGUE
Visions

In that uncharted territory between consciousness and sleep, just before thoughts throttle down and the brain turns off, my overactive mind sends images that flash into my semi-consciousness. Sometimes they have substance and sometimes not. Often, they reflect what is on my mind.

I envision a baby-faced teammate with a combed-out afro sitting directly across from me, holding a basketball and leaning forward to speak. The intensity in his fiery brown eyes gives me pause. Initially, I am intimidated, unsure how to respond. But the energy he exudes burns through my personal space. It lights a fire in my belly and instills fearlessness and confidence. I am ready!

I imagine my father, a naïve, idealistic young man, churning across the ocean to Japan, our country's recently defeated enemy and now an occupied territory. Upon landing, I sense he is heartbroken by the utter destruction and human tragedy that surround him. I wonder how he will navigate the bureaucratic morass of the Army and land a position playing football. I catch a reflection of his face in the glass as he gazes out a train window at the scarred interior of Japan. He is homesick, though positive about the future and appreciative of his good fortune.

I picture a teenaged Civil War soldier, small in stature, proudly wearing his Union blues over ragged home-sewn garments and worn boots. He struggles with his 55-pound pack, hungry and scared, trying to keep up with fellow soldiers as they trudge through the woods from one encampment to another. His face reflects an air of weary innocence as his eyes dart nervously from side to side. He is not yet battle tested. He has never strayed from his small homestead in rural Ohio, and he misses his family and questions his resolve.

I feel the thumping vibrations of an incoming helicopter speeding over a desolate wasteland carrying a cargo of Army Ranger grunts in its belly. Their mission: to maneuver through the thick jungle, off the grid, and search for an enemy—one that is seasoned in guerilla warfare, ubiquitous but invisible in the surrounding uninhabitable landscape.

I see savior pilots and crewmen brazenly spiraling down in their Hueys through the hail of small arms fire and exploding mortars into hot landing zones to rescue fellow warriors from the carnage of Vietnam. I sense the relief and gratitude of their passengers as they are lifted out of harm's way.

Drifting off to sleep, these words are my final thought: *Let us not forget those who have preceded and supported us, fought for our freedom, displayed unparalleled courage, made us who we are, and hardwired themselves to our hearts.*

ROAD WORTHY

ROAD
WORTHY

PART 1

PART I

CHAPTER 1
The Mallet

There are a few select days in my life that I can remember with complete clarity, from beginning to end, as if they were yesterday. Saturday, February 8, 1975, was one of those days. I was seventeen years old, one of the stars on my high school's basketball team, a shy, gangly, long-haired kid playing mostly with and against hardened kids from the tougher parts of town. My biggest fan, though he never gave me much positive reinforcement, was my dad.

My dad was a former teacher and football coach turned lawyer. He knew football inside and out, and he understood coaching. I guess, since he possessed these skills and since I was his son, he felt he knew better than anyone, including me, what I needed to do to succeed in basketball. I'm not sure I ever reached his highest expectation, achieved that perfect game, though he attended every game I played from sixth through twelfth grade. Unfortunately, and to my regret now, he forgot how to relate to me once I became a teenager. I didn't know how to relate to him either, so the slight unease or discomfort we experienced around each other through my high school years and beyond was equally shared. Parents of that generation did not really talk to their kids. The boundaries were too distinct. My dad did not know how to give me praise. Either that or from his Army and coaching days he felt that criticism was a better motivational tool. Some nights after games, I was afraid to come home because I knew I'd get an earful as soon as I crossed the threshold of our front door.

That Saturday, I awakened to my dad banging on my bedroom door yelling, "The pressure's on." I had no idea what he was referring to or why he was bothering me at such an early hour, especially since I had a game that night against our arch-rival Pompano Beach, the other top team in our conference.

It turns out my dad had gotten up at 7 am and read the *Fort Lauderdale Sun Sentinel*, Broward County's main newspaper. On the front of the sports page, there was a story about our upcoming evening game with a picture of me. I had missed the earlier matchup against Pompano Beach because I had the flu. The Tornados had crushed us. The point of this morning's story was that I was back, completely recovered, and that it would be a more even playing field. My mom told me my dad sat at the table watching the clock, barely able to contain himself for two hours. Thankfully, she insisted he let me sleep in.

By 9 am, my dad could restrain himself no longer. He stood outside my door banging and hollering. I tried to ignore him, pulled pillows over my head, but he would not let up. I stumbled out of bed to see what he was so excited about. I opened my bedroom door and found him standing there with a big smile on his face. He immediately blurted, "It's all up to you tonight."

He grabbed my arm and pulled me out to the dining room where the paper was sitting on the table. I sat down and gazed at the sports page spread out in front of me. I saw my face with a silly half smile next to the caption, "Deerfield Battles Pompano Tonight." Word for word, the article read:

"The fans know it's a biggie. They showed it by buying out the gym for tonight's Deerfield-Pompano Beach game early in the week. All 1200 seats are gone, and none will be sold at the door. Pompano was allotted 300 student tickets and 100 adult tickets.

The visiting Tornadoes (21-2) lead Deerfield by a full game in the Northern Division of the Broward County Athletic Conference. Pompano has a 12-1 division record after its victory over Dillard, and Deerfield, 19-3 overall, is 11-2 in the BCAC.

The two teams met earlier in the season with Pompano getting an easier than expected 83-63 win. Deerfield, though, was playing without Jimmy Ziegler, the Bucks' 6-foot 3 junior post, possibly the most stabilizing element the team has.

He was also out when the Bucks lost to Leonard and did not play in the first half of Deerfield's game with Boyd Anderson when the Bucks trailed by nine at intermission. He returned in the second half to lead his team to a going away victory.

The Bucks also have the county's leading scorer in guard Jimmy Morgan, who sports a 29.3 point per game average. Deerfield could pretty much eliminate itself by losing, falling two games back with just two games to play."

I finished the article, and with typical teenage aloofness and a pretense of disinterest, I looked into the kitchen and asked my mom, "What's for breakfast?" I think my dad expected a bigger response, but the newspaper story didn't faze me. I felt certain we would be a different team that night.

My mom made me a toasted peanut butter and lettuce sandwich, a staple in our household, and I strolled into the backyard and sat down on one of our lawn chairs. My dad had picked several grapefruit earlier that morning, and I heard the juicer whirring as he made fresh juice. He brought me out a tall glass. I lounged in the South Florida sun and finished my breakfast.

That Saturday was one of those rare, high pressure, low humidity Florida days with a clear blue sky and a slight west wind. The air was cool but warm in the sun. Mourning doves lined the telephone wire outside our house and cooed their morning ritual. The smell of citrus and fresh cut grass prompted me to lay back with my feet up and close my eyes. I thought about the newspaper article and my unlikely journey over the previous two years following my father's abrupt decision to move our family from a small town in northwestern Ohio to South Florida's Gold Coast. I felt like I'd been torn away from everything familiar, including my extended family and all my friends.

The transition was difficult, and the first few months in my new, ethnically diverse high school were challenging. Since I was a new student, the guidance department assigned me to remedial or "college prep" courses. In the early seventies, racial tensions ran high, and in some classes, I sensed an undercurrent of hostility between certain classmates. Occasionally, fights broke out. My only salvation, outside of my immediate family, was basketball.

I thought back to early November of my freshman year, my first day reporting to try-outs. I was good, but I knew no one and had not played with anyone in town. As I entered the gym, a sea of unfriendly faces looked up at me, in my mind disdainfully asking, "what in the hell was I doing on their turf?"

There was one kid standing at mid-court talking with Mike Benanti, the JV coach, and he was the only one who was smiling. From across the gym, this kid radiated confidence. I was tall for a freshman, already 6' 2". This kid was about 5' 11", rock solid, and my first thought was that he looked more like a fullback or middle linebacker than a basketball player. I soon discovered he was an exceptional player, one with no limitations. His name was Jimmy Morgan. He was a year ahead of me, and he was the only sophomore swinging between the JV and the stacked varsity, a team predicted to win Broward County the coming year and ranked in the pre-season top ten in the state of Florida.

Coach Benanti had gotten wind of a new kid in school who might be able to play basketball. Because of my height, he invited me to try out for the JV team. Only one other freshman, Calvin "Magic" Hannah had been invited, but Calvin was still playing football that day, so he was not in the gym. The coach smiled at me and said, "Get a ball and warm up."

There were games of 3 on 3 at both ends of the main court, with most of the coach's attention focused on the kids playing at the eastern end. I grabbed a ball and jogged to one of the side baskets and took a few shots. I noticed the solid kid at half court turn to watch me. I was flustered, my insecurity heightened by the awareness that "Mr. Confidence" was watching. Part of me wanted to run out of that gym.

After a few minutes, action stopped on the eastern end, and Coach Benanti called over to me and two others to jump in and play the winners. I was tentative, more worried about making a mistake than asserting myself. Play began. I was guarding a kid my height with uncanny moves, seemingly in slow motion but very hard to anticipate and stop. During one possession, a player on the other team took a shot. As I boxed out my opponent, I felt a hard elbow to the small of my back and was pushed out of bounds. I turned and watched my opponent snag the rebound and score. Instead of getting pissed at what was clearly a flagrant foul, I felt more intimidated.

Coach Benanti sensed I was rattled and yelled out, "Hey, why don't you guys take a quick water break and then come back in and finish?"

I wasn't thirsty, but the other five players filed out of the gym to the drinking fountain in the lobby. I stared blankly at the basket and took a few shots. One careened off the rim and rolled off the court. The confident, solid guy chased it down, but instead of

5

passing it to me, he slowly walked over and placed the ball in my hands. He stared into my eyes and asked, "What's your name?"

I replied, "Jim."

"What's your last name?"

I told him, "Ziegler."

He responded, "My name is Hook and from now on, I'm callin' you Z. You gotta quit letting that pussy push you around out there. Next time you get the ball, if he gets up on you, take him to the hole; if he backs off, put it in his eye. And if he pushes you, push him right back."

I could feel the intensity in Hook's eyes as he held my gaze. At first, I was terrified, but then I looked around. I noticed the gym was silent, everyone watching the two of us. It made me think that Hook did not necessarily waste his time interacting with just anyone on the basketball court. I glanced once more into his eyes, and my confidence returned.

When play resumed, I lost my tentativeness. I took my opponent to the hole, and when he backed off, I put a couple fifteen to eighteen footers "in his eye." When his teammates started focusing on me, I dished to my teammates. We won that half-court scrimmage, and at the end, Coach Benanti said, "Welcome to my JV team."

As I walked out of the gym that first day, Hook caught up with me, and under his breath said, "You and me; we're gonna rule this county in two years." He turned out to be right, though we had some help from a few friends, and his contribution to our "greatness" was significantly more than mine.

I returned to the present, moved my chair into the shade, and on that most perfect South Florida winter day, stretched out and fell asleep. Next thing I knew, someone was shaking my arm trying to wake me up. Initially, I thought it was my little brother, Joe, but when I opened my eyes, I saw my dad standing above me with a guilty look on his face.

He bent over and quietly said, "C'mon, let's go get some lunch."

My mom had recently gone on a nutrition kick that included ingesting vinegar, taking multiple vitamins and supplements, and fasting one day a week. My poor father was her primary test subject. Though he'd shed some extra pounds around his mid-section, he was not thrilled with the new diet, which changed weekly. His look told me that we were sneaking out of the house to go eat some real food, which meant we were heading to his favorite get-away, McDonalds. On a big game day, I think we both felt we could justify it. I walked through the house to grab my keys while my dad snuck around outside to meet me in the front. Since I was new to driving, we had an understanding that we'd drive my car any time he and I traveled together.

We got into my four-door olive green 1969 Chevy Biscayne that I'd inherited from my grandparents. It was a tank of a car, in my memory eight feet wide and fifteen to twenty feet long, comfortably able to accommodate three grown men in each seat with at least two feet of head room. It sported a massive hood in front and an equally capacious trunk in back. Transmission was manual, "three on the tree," and though it accelerated like a drunk turtle, once it had momentum, it could probably take a semi head-on and come out little worse for wear.

As I turned the key in the ignition, my killer new combination 8-track tape and FM stereo sound system blasted out of the rear coaxial speakers startling both of us. At that age, I had only one volume for playing music—LOUD. Instinctively, I turned the sound down, aware of my dad's dislike of rock and roll, just "noise" as he referred to it. Elton John's version of the Beatles' *Lucy in the Sky with Diamonds* was playing on the radio, and though I loved Elton's original work, I loved the Beatles more. I felt "Lucy" was one piece that Elton should not be singing. I turned the stereo off.

Though my dad and I enjoyed each other's company, because of the void in relating to one another, when it was just the two of us, we rarely looked at each other or said much. That Saturday, I pulled out of our neighborhood and went west on Hillsboro Boulevard, the main east-west throughway in Deerfield Beach. I then took a quick left to head south on Route 1, which at the time was a four-lane highway divided by a grass median with traffic lights poorly synchronized every quarter mile or so. Both of us stared ahead, lost in thought, windows open, elbows sticking out. I think we were equally excited about the evening's game, feeling that on a day like this, there was really no reason to talk anyway.

We passed multiple small strip malls, the plaza housing my father's law office, a few car dealerships, and some bigger new shopping centers. The sun was directly overhead. It warmed the inside of my "tank" and shined on both of our tanned protruding forearms. Traffic was heavy, mostly with all the transient "snowbirds" from up north wintering in South Florida.

We approached the old-style Golden Arches, which had a large neon sign out front bragging about the number of hamburgers sold to date. We pulled in, parked, got out, and lazily walked up to the serving window.

At this McDonalds, there was no inside seating. Outdoor tables were scattered in front, some with raised umbrellas. Most customers grabbed their food, scurried back to their cars, ate, or rode on. No one was in line at the serving window, so we walked up, and my dad ordered a Big Mac, large fries, and a large chocolate milk shake. I was impressed by his rebellious spirit!

We enjoyed our lunches at one of the outdoor tables, mostly in silence. My dad asked me a few questions about the game which I'm sure I annoyingly responded to with grunts or one-word answers. Funny, now forty-plus years later, as a father of two, I so clearly understand that "what goes around, comes around."

We finished eating, headed back to my car, and pulled out. We continued south on Route 1, away from home, as there was no break in the median to turn north. A few hundred yards from McDonalds, there was a run-down duplex strip mall with a dilapidated thrift shop and a dingy used record store next to it. No cars were parked in front of either store. My dad excitedly instructed me to take a right. Always the collector and treasure hunter, I knew this meant at least a thirty-minute detour as he carefully rummaged for a hidden gem amongst the junk in the thrift shop. I begrudgingly pulled in, and he jumped out of the car. He looked back at me.

"You comin' in?" he asked.

"I'll wait," I replied.

I turned on my 8-track tape player and lost myself in Elton John's *Goodbye Yellow Brick Road*. I watched my father through the window of the thrift shop, the only customer carefully perusing items as he slowly walked up and down the aisles. He appeared completely immersed in his search for another great "find." I glanced over at the record store, which had an outside box full of 8-track cassettes marked "SALE." I turned off the ignition and walked over to the bin. I rifled through the tapes and found *Who's Next* by the Who, one of my favorite albums of all time, priced at $1.29. I only had a dollar, so I walked into the thrift store and borrowed 29 cents from my dad. He was so thrilled with an item he had found that he didn't ask me what the money was for.

I purchased the cassette, walked back to my car, pushed the tape into my player, cranked the volume, and sat waiting for my dad. A few minutes later, he emerged from the thrift shop. He was whistling, clearly very pleased with his find. He held a small paper bag. I turned off the stereo, and after he got into the car, backed up and pulled out to the end of the parking lot. I looked over and asked my dad what he'd bought. Just as he began to answer, a copper colored Le Mans screamed past, well over the speed limit, with its horn blasting. It was Kevin, one of my best friends and the second-string center on our high school basketball team. As he blew by, he screamed out the window, "Z, you da man."

A few seconds later, we watched a police car, lights flashing, pass by, catch up to Kevin, and pull him over. I found out later that Kevin received two tickets that day, one for speeding and one for "illegal use of horn."

The moment passed, and we exited the small parking lot back onto the highway. I smiled at Kevin as I passed his car on the side of the road, the cop car's lights flashing behind him. I noted his defeated look, which turned to panic when he realized my dad was in the passenger's seat of my car. A short distance past Kevin, I made a U-turn and retraced our route north. I forgot about the small paper bag my dad was holding.

When we got home, my dad asked me to hose off the lawn mower I'd used to cut the grass the evening before. It was now mid-afternoon, and the sun was starting its descent to the west. I would be leaving for the high school in a few hours. I first went into the house, through the kitchen, to my room. I passed my dad with his mid-day vitamins and supplements lined up on the counter next to a small glass of apple cider vinegar. I smiled at him. My dad gazed back with a defeated look. He knew that noncompliance with my mother's newly honed nutritional expertise, mostly learned from infomercials, was not an option. Though she was kind, empathetic, and altruistic, almost to a fault, my petite little mom also had a stubborn streak that could not be breached. We simply did not question some things in our house. Luckily, since I was an athlete and burning so many calories, my mom allowed me to eat a typical teenage diet. She only insisted I take a few multivitamins each day. At the time, the vinegar kick was only between my mom and her main test subject, my dad.

I walked into my bedroom, which was decorated in vintage 'seventies motif—bright red walls, red shag carpeting, huge stereo system with stand-up speakers, and posters of athletes and rock stars on the walls. My dad didn't believe in wasting his hard-earned money on air conditioning, so I surrounded my bed with fans which blew from all angles, augmented by a ceiling fan directly overhead for hot, sticky, summer nights.

My mom called out to me from the kitchen, "Jimmy, grab your uniform from the dryer and pack your bag for the game. Dad and I are heading to the office for a few hours to finish some work." She asked me to keep an eye out for my 10-year-old brother, Joe, who was fishing somewhere in the neighborhood and my 13-year-old sister, Edie, who was off with friends.

I packed my red and gold gym bag, emblazoned with "Deerfield Beach Bucks," walked out our front door, and threw it onto the rear seat of my car. I then went to the back of our house and grabbed the lawn mower which I'd left under an awning the night before. Our house was typical old-Florida: a single floor, sprawling ranch with a large screened-in patio and pool. I pushed the mower around to our side yard and grabbed the hose and uncoiled it from its holder. I was about to turn it on when I heard distant giggling erupt into laughter. I looked up and saw my sister Edie and her best friend Gail slowly walking up the street. They were returning from the beach, still dressed in their bathing suits.

Only in eighth grade, my sister Edie was already a beautiful teenager with long golden-blonde hair. Her friend Gail had bright auburn hair, and together they looked like two classic beauties, salt and pepper, with mischief in their eyes. They were all about fun and laughed nonstop, easily amused by each other's antics. That day, framed by the blue sky, their hair sparkled in the sun.

I turned on the hose and started spraying the mower. My sister and Gail walked over to where I was standing, and Gail said, "Edie, I didn't know Mr. Cool had to lower himself to do routine work around the house."

I was not going to give them the satisfaction of acknowledging Gail's comment. I finished hosing off the mower, changed the

11

nozzle head from spray to soak mode, looked up at the two of them, and said, "Nice to see you too Gail." I then soaked both of them with water. They turned and ran screaming and laughing into the house.

I rolled the lawn mower to the garage and tried to enter the house through the door from the garage. Locked. I walked around to the front door and tried the handle. Locked. I knocked on the door, rang the doorbell, and yelled at Edie. No response. I walked around back and entered the screened-in patio and pool area. The sliding glass doors into the living and dining rooms were locked. I looked at the window over the kitchen sink, and though it was closed, I could tell it wasn't locked.

I hatched a plan. I exited the patio area and went to the front door and screamed at Edie to open it. No response. I waited a few minutes and then crept back around the house quietly re-entering the patio area. I crawled over to the kitchen window. I could hear Elton John's *Levon* blasting inside so I figured Edie and Gail were in her room. I stood up and slowly opened the window leading into the kitchen. It gave me about ten inches to maneuver through. I silently hoisted myself onto the outside shelf and started shimmying through the window, into the kitchen, my head face down over the kitchen sink. Just as I was beginning to feel very proud of my genius plan of entry, Gail jumped up from in front of the sink with a bucket of water and poured it over my head. Edie then grabbed the nozzle used to hose off dishes and sprayed me as I made a quick retreat through the window, back onto the patio. The two of them gazed out at me, so thoroughly overjoyed with their victory that they could barely stand up as they laughed mercilessly at my expense. They quickly closed the kitchen window and locked it.

I exited the patio and couldn't help but laugh as I walked back around to the front of the house. I knocked on the door and heard Edie stop laughing and sarcastically reply, "Who is it?"

"It's your dumbass big brother. Who the hell do you think it is?"

"What do you want?" she asked.

"I need to come in and get ready for my game," I responded.

"Oh. You have a big game tonight? Who's your favorite sister?"

"You are."

Gail then interjected, "Who's the coolest eighth grader you know?"

I knew they had me, so I had to say, "You are Gail."

Edie then said, "Swear to God that we are even and that you aren't going to do anything to us."

"I swear we are even, and I'm not going to do anything to you."

Edie replied, "You gotta swear to God." She knew that the only one I was more afraid of than my father was God, and in our family, swearing to God was an irrevocable commitment, assurance that she and Gail were safe from any recourse on my part.

I was out of options. "Ok, I swear to God we are even. I will not do anything to you."

After a few seconds, I heard the door unlock. I pulled it open and was greeted by the very satisfied faces of Edie and Gail, their arms crossed, wicked little grins proclaiming victory at my expense. Water dripped off me as I brushed past them to my room.

It was now close to 4 pm, and the shadows outside were growing longer. I showered and ate my pre-game meal. I had to be at the high school by 6:15 pm, stow my gear in the locker room, and then sit with my teammates for the JV game, which began at 6:30 pm. Varsity tip-off was scheduled for 8 pm.

My parents returned from the office, and my mom bustled about the kitchen making dinner for my dad, Edie and Gail, and my brother, Joe, who had just returned from fishing with his little pack of neighborhood friends. As the five of them sat down for dinner, I went to my room to complete my pre-game ritual, listening to Todd Rundgren's song *Just One Victory*. I put on earphones, turned up the volume, and sat on the edge of my bed. The words of the refrain put me into game mode.

"Pray for it all day, and fight for it all night, give us just one victory, it will be all right." The lyrics seemed to speak to me and ignite a fire in my belly. Funny, I never listened to that song once I stopped playing high school basketball, but I can still hear that refrain in my head.

When it was time to leave, I grabbed my keys and walked out to my car. Calls of "good luck" and "kick some butt" echoed in my ears. I exited our neighborhood, turned west on Hillsboro Blvd, and drove straight into bright shades of yellow and orange hovering over the western horizon.

After a mile or so, I crossed the railroad tracks and turned south onto Dixie Highway. My Black teammates lived west of Dixie Highway. Back then, there was a distinct demarcation between whites and Blacks in Deerfield Beach: the railroad tracks that ran north to south. One did not see many Blacks east of the tracks except to work, and few whites ventured into the Black neighborhoods.

Though the homes were not as elaborate here as in some of the wealthier parts of town, there were always lots of people milling about, interacting with their neighbors. As I drove by, people recognized my car and waved or gave me a thumbs up.

As I continued south on Dixie Highway toward Deerfield Beach High School, I thought back to my team's journey and its improbable run to become one of the elite high school basketball teams in Broward County and the State of Florida. Our team centered around Jimmy, the only senior of the starting five. He was the heart, soul, and leader. I was Jimmy's sidekick. Before every game, he would come over, sit directly in front of me, stare me down, and ask, "Z, you ready?" If he sensed any doubt or hesitation in my game face or reply, he'd ask me again, "Z, you ready?" He would not let up until satisfied I was "ready."

I played the wing and averaged just under eighteen points per game. Our other wing was Greg Robinson. Smooth as silk, he effortlessly floated over the floor. Greg was usually mild-mannered, always smiling, but he was fearless and would not back down from anyone. Push him too hard and he would get right in your face. He averaged thirteen points per game. Our point guard was Calvin "Magic" Hannah. Calvin was "Magic" before Magic was Magic. The girls thought he was dreamy, but anyone who played ball with him knew he was truly magic. Calvin was lightening quick, stealthy, and he could jump out of the gym. He never spoke on the court, could have averaged twenty points per game if he wanted to, but he much preferred running the point and making others look good.

The four of us had played together the year before, but we were young, inexperienced, and we didn't have a big man. We had not had a good year. The summer before my junior year, two things happened that cemented our destiny. First, the four of us played together every day—in gyms, outside in the scorching summer sun, on courts in the white neighborhoods, on courts in the Black neighborhoods. It didn't matter. We got to know each other's "games" as well as we knew our own. Second, a kid who had played JV the previous year, Al Beal, grew five inches and was 6 foot 9 inches as we entered summer. Al was thin, not particularly strong, and very soft. But he had long arms and could jump. Jimmy and I knew he was our ticket to playing at the next level. The four of us started making Al join us each day, sometimes pleading with him to get his ass off the couch and come out into the miserable, humid Florida heat. By the end of summer, Al was battle tested and protected the rim like an assassin. By mid-fall of my junior year, we felt certain our team was going to be a force. No one outside our little circle knew, and pre-season polls had us finishing dead last in the Broward County Northern Division.

Things changed rapidly after we won our first thirteen games, blowing some teams out by the end of the first quarter. We began selling out every home game, and our boisterous fans packed gyms even when we played away. I smiled to myself. Team members (including myself) had become minor celebrities around town.

I reached the high school entrance and carefully pulled in past a cop directing traffic. It was only 6:15 pm, almost dark, and the parking lot was already filling up. I saw a long line of people extending from the gym entrance snaking down an outside hallway past the cafeteria into the parking lot. I walked past the line of people, some of whom expected they would be able to buy a ticket at the door.

I slid through a side door, carefully closing it behind me. Silence. Nervous anticipation. For the first time all day, I realized that this was a big game. The conference championship was on the line, and the whole town was coming out. It was "make or break" time.

I walked twenty feet or so and took a left into an adjoining hallway that ended with the locker room door on the left and the back entrance to the gym on the right. The JV team was warming up, and I heard noise coming from inside the gym. As I approached the locker room entrance, Mr. Weigel, our athletic director, came barreling out the door to make his way into the gym. He looked up and saw me, stopped, smiled, and in his raspy voice said, "Ooohhhh, if it isn't the Z-man with his girly long blonde hair. Your poor father! But you are the greatest thing since toilet paper, now aren't you?"

Pleased with his humorous remarks, he then continued to the gym. As he grabbed the door handle, he abruptly stopped and glanced back at me. It was the first time I'd ever seen Mr. Weigel serious. With a steady but stern voice he admonished me, "Z, go out there and kick the pants off those arrogant a-holes. Show them how a real team plays." Before I could respond, he yanked the door open and disappeared into the gym.

I strolled into the locker room to stash my gear. I then entered the gym and sat down next to my best friend Mark, our sixth man. Kevin, who I'd last seen earlier that day pulled over by a policeman,

16

sat next to Mark. The two of them were part of my closest friend group, "the golden seven," so named by Kevin. The rest of our team stretched out in the rows in front and behind us. Each team member looked at me and nodded or smiled. Hook gave me his signature wink. The only one missing was Lamar, our second-string point guard. Lamar was Hook's best friend, so I leaned forward and asked him, "Where's Lamar?"

Hook replied, "That crazy ass got ahold of ten tickets for the game and he's out in the parking lot trying to scalp them." In my mind, I pictured Lamar, the consummate salesman, racking up a lot of green.

Only a few minutes into the junior varsity game, I was a bit surprised to see the gym more than half-filled and people continuing to stream in at a steady pace. The atmosphere was electric. My eyes swept the home stands on the other side of the gym, and I noted other members of the "golden seven" seated in various locations. As each of them caught my eye, they gave me a thumbs up or a fist, letting me know they each had my back. On the far-right side, about ten rows up from the floor, sat Arlan Birkman with two of his friends. Arlan was a teacher at the Lutheran school affiliated with the church my family attended. He had just started dating my older sister, Ellen. Our eyes locked briefly, and he smiled and gave me a thumbs up. To the left of Arlan sat our raucous student body. They were already going at it, cheering the JV team and objecting to every call the referees made.

I gazed toward the main entrance of the gym as my parents walked through the doors with my little brother Joe followed by Mark's parents, Jim and Judy Montgomery, and then Edie and Gail. My dad and Mr. Montgomery, both imposing, handsome men, looked like they could be NFL middle linebackers. They had designated seats, top row, direct middle on the home side. No one dared sit in those seats, and usually no one ventured too close to the two of them. During sold out games, the only place where the wood of the stands was visible was next to my father and "Big Jim."

As the two men climbed to their designated spots, I watched my mom and Mrs. Montgomery try to find seats as far away from their husbands as possible. My brother separated from my parents and joined my high school friends in the student section, "little Z" feeling like a king among the sea of rowdy teenage students. Edie and Gail sat by themselves.

As I surveyed the other side of the gym, I experienced a momentary awareness that this was a special evening. For a few hours, all was and would be right within my insulated little world. I had everyone and everything I needed: family, friends, teammates, youth, health, trust in the future. As I look back now, 42 years later, I realize how truly blessed I was at that moment. My parents, alive and in the prime of their lives. Arlan, with his mischievous blue eyes and snickering laugh, on cloud nine, madly in love with my sister. My siblings, all young, happy, and healthy. A group of close-knit friends with that tight connection that only exists when going through transformative years together. My teammates, unique guys who shared an intense bond built from battling together with a common purpose. I was truly at peace, and all these years later I can still recapture the feelings of innocence, contentedness, and anticipation. I can visualize the faces in that crowd and sense the web of support many of those people provided. I can even feel the cool dry air of that perfect Florida evening that was filtering into the gym.

Strangely, the one thing about that day I don't remember much about is the actual game. I do remember flashes. Before the game, Coach Benanti stormed around the locker room yelling, "Where the hell is Lamar?" I remember Lamar running in, his pockets filled with cash, and quickly changing right before we went onto the floor. On one of the first possessions, I remember trailing a three-on-two fast break with Jimmy handling the ball in the middle and Greg Robinson on the left wing. As the two defenders keyed on

Jimmy, he dished a perfect behind-the-back bounce pass to Greg. Greg flew toward the rim, made the lay-up, and then took a hard foul from Pompano's 6', 8" big man well after scoring. This led to a bench clearing near-brawl and an emptying of the stands onto the court. My dad jumped in front of Greg to prevent fists from flying, and things cooled down and the court cleared. For some reason, the refs threw Greg out of the game but no one from Pompano's team. I thought Coach Benanti was going to blow a gasket, but he collected himself, and as Jimmy and I walked Greg off the court to the door leading to the locker room, Coach Benanti signaled Mark to check into the game.

As we reached the gym door, Jimmy glared at Greg and then me and quietly proclaimed, "They do not stand a chance now." I had never seen Jimmy more resolute, and I felt empowered. I quickly affirmed, "Greg, this one's for you." I remember that instant, feeling as a trio, soon to be down to a duo, that we were invincible. Greg, with tears in his eyes and a look of helplessness, yanked open the gym door and disappeared into the dark hallway. Jimmy and I turned and walked back onto the court.

I remember with seconds left at the end of the first half flashing to the top of the key, receiving a perfect pass from Magic, and shooting a turn-around jumper that hit nothing but net as the buzzer sounded. As I ran off the court to the locker room at halftime, Mr. Weigel grabbed me and lifted me off my feet with a suffocating bear hug. We led by eight points at the half and never relinquished that lead.

Near the end of the game, Pompano had to resort to fouling, and I stepped to the line twice in the final ninety seconds of the game with one and ones. With complete confidence, I made all four foul shots. The second time, as the referee handed me the ball, one of Pompano's players (a supposed friend of mine off the court), looked at me and said, "Hey Z, I been meaning to tell you that you ain't shit." As I sank the first shot, I caught his eyes and smiled. As I made the second, I thought to myself, "Chew on that you loser."

When the game ended, the fans flocked onto the gym floor and hoisted us up. I again remember looking around at all those loving faces, my parents, my brother, my sister, Arlan, my best friends, fists pumping, smiles on their faces. Springsteen sings about "Glory days, they pass you by," and they do, but that was a glorious day, and though my father and Arlan are no longer alive, I can see their faces and sense their presence when I think back to that night. I knew then and I know now that I was fortunate to have that experience and especially blessed to have those people in my life. When you are young, you don't realize that you will soon be old, that those people dearest to your heart will gradually thin in number. I look at my daughters now, and they still think I'm invincible; that I will always be around. I am terrified to know that I won't, that they will not always have that background cloak of loving support and protection.

After the game, my parents opened our home to my teammates and their families. We had a wildly jubilant crowd fill our house. After the last guest left that night, I walked into my bedroom and felt the night breeze blowing through my windows. There was a slight chill to the air, and I realized this would be a "no fan" night. I strolled out to the kitchen to make a bedtime snack and saw my dad sitting on the sofa in the living room with the small paper bag from the thrift shop. I went over and sat down next to him.

I asked him, "What did you actually buy at that thrift shop today?"

My father handed me a light object, a wooden mallet. The handle was about a foot long and a third of an inch in diameter very gradually tapering as it attached to a three to four-inch rectangular head that then rounded on each end. A thin outer lining of copper encased the two rounded ends. I saw shallowly engraved writing on the front and back of the rectangular head. It was illegible on one side but clearly said "Andersonville Ga." on the other. The object appeared very old, dirty, and delicate, the work of a careful and patient whittler.

My dad glanced over at me and said, "Not bad for a quarter, eh?"

I asked him, "Where is Andersonville, Ga?"

My dad, somewhat of a history buff, explained to me that Andersonville was a notorious Civil War prisoner of war (POW) camp in the heart of southern Georgia. It was a place where Confederate guards packed Union soldiers inside a stockade fence and left them to fend for themselves, exposed, with little food and no clean water. It was a place known for disease, starvation, suffering, and death. It represented an especially sordid chapter in a war that killed more Americans than any other.

I asked. "Do you think the mallet was made there, during the Civil War?"

"I don't know," he replied as he twirled it in his hands.

He then stood up, looked down at me, and said, "Crazy day today."

My mom had already retired to bed. As my father reached their bedroom door, he paused, turned, and said, "That was some game tonight." He then opened the door, disappeared into his room, and softly closed it behind him.

I walked to my room, climbed into bed, and pulled a sheet over me. I thought back to the game as I fell asleep. I completely forgot about the mallet. For thirty years, my dad mostly did too.

CHAPTER 2
My Father, Nicholas J. Ziegler

According to my father, his life did not begin at birth. For him, he'd say, life really began when he was fourteen. He was returning home on a late Sunday afternoon in early December after a day of skating at the *Rollercade*, the best roller-skating rink in Cleveland, Ohio. As he walked the city streets toward home, his skates tied together and slung over his shoulder, it felt like any other late fall weekend afternoon—the air clear and brisk, little auto traffic, and periodic clanging of street trolley bells. Lost in thought, he looked forward to the evening meal in his tight-knit household, feeling safe because all was right in his little world.

Suddenly a man he didn't know or recognize grabbed him by the shoulders. My father turned and faced the man, and it was obvious that this stranger wanted to share something important.

"Have you heard the news?" the man blurted out.

"What news?" my dad replied.

"Japan has bombed Pearl Harbor," he declared.

My dad had no idea where Pearl Harbor was or the significance of the bombing, but he could tell from the man's voice and the look on the man's face that this event was serious.

Within hours of the Japanese attack on Pearl Harbor, Germany declared war on the United States. The innocent sense of peace and safety that my dad assumed would last forever was shattered. His country was now fighting two enemies on two major fronts, and there was a gnawing fear that our great nation could be overpowered. Under this ominous cloud, my father finished his sophomore year of high school.

My dad was named Nicholas Jacob, the first name taken from his father. I do not know where "Jacob" came from. He grew up in a rundown section of downtown Cleveland. His family rented the second floor of a double on a busy street with traffic noise and street cars screeching outside the windows. He lived with his parents, his older sister Betty, and his mother's parents who he referred to as Muttie and Vatti. His mother's sister, Theresa, lived with them when he was young. His parents were first generation German-Americans, and the grandparents who lived in the house did not speak English.

My dad's father loved America and all it stood for. Although he had many relatives in the old country, my grandfather never went back to visit. Though fluent in German, he never spoke it outside the home. According to my father, his dad felt he had everything he needed in America. There was no reason to visit the land of his ancestors.

My dad did not say much else about his family; in fact, I can't recall him ever volunteering information about his parents without prodding—significant prodding! His mother died young when my dad was in his twenties, and I never met her. His father died when I was a young child. I have a vague memory of going to visit him shortly before my grandfather's death. Together, my father and I climbed rickety outdoor stairs into a smoky house that smelled damp and musty. We stayed for a short visit, and I don't think I even went into the bedroom to see my grandfather. Months later, I remember accompanying my dad to visit his father's grave. It was a bone-chilling overcast day, and my father was silent on the ride to the cemetery and then the entire way back. When we returned home, he thanked me for going with him. At the time, I thought his silence in the car reflected sadness, though I was confused as to why he had asked me along. Perhaps, the loss of his parent was tempered by the innocence and potential of me, his son.

My father's upbringing profoundly affected him in a way that made him very rigid when it came to career choices, politics, personal accountability, and acceptable behavior. If you crossed him or displayed a character trait he disapproved of, you lost his respect, and it was difficult to gain it back. He had no time for people he didn't respect. His ambition, which seems a bit reckless looking back, was fueled by a constant desire to better himself, create an exceptional life for his wife and children, and escape the urban blight in which he grew up. His politics reflected his fierce independence. He was a self-made man, never asking anyone for anything, and he didn't believe in handouts, especially government sponsored. His father was a company man, active in his union, living paycheck to paycheck. My dad hated the thought of working for "the man" and paying dues to unions. He felt they were corrupt organizations existing only to fund their bureaucracies. When I was growing up, he constantly advised me to get good grades, graduate college, and then go to professional school, preferably medical or law.

My dad was a good athlete, tough and fearless. He played football growing up, though mostly sandlot without any formal instruction or coaching. Fistfights frequently broke out on the playgrounds of Cleveland, and I know my father was pummeled to the point of unconsciousness on more than one occasion. As a junior at West Tech High School, he tried out for the football team. He was thrilled when the coach awarded him a uniform, but because he had no real training, he was relegated to the "scrubs" or as he described them, the "rinky dinks."

My father once informed me that over my lifetime I would meet "angels," people who'd show up at pivotal moments, with no agenda, and offer timely help or guidance, expecting nothing in return. He told me to always listen to these individuals, that I would know it when I was in their presence. My father's first encounter with "angels" occurred during his junior year of high school while at football practice. It was a bleak fall day, and he was on the sidelines with the other scrubs watching the first team players go at it. Out of frustration, he intermittently walked over to the blocking sled and gave it a smack.

Two men, one in a plaid shirt and one in a sailor's uniform, walked up to the fence surrounding the practice field and called him over to them. The two men made suggestions about blocking, stance, footwork, balance, and gaining the advantage. For the next thirty minutes, these two men coached my father, teaching him the fundamentals of standing up blockers, avoiding getting trapped, and tackling the ball carrier. The head coach of the football team watched out of the corner of his eye but said nothing as he continued to work with the first team. The coach finally blew his whistle: time to scrimmage.

He yelled out to my father, "Ziegler, get in there at defensive tackle."

The two men walked to the sidelines and continued instructing my father. The first offensive play came his way, and my father stood up the pulling guard and tackled the ball carrier in the backfield.

The men continued shouting instructions, "Stay low, use your forearms, keep your hands ready, be patient, deliver the blow."

And on it went. The coach ran play after play at my father, and he stopped everything. At the end of scrimmage, my father

25

looked over at the sidelines, and the two men were gone. He never saw them again.

That Friday, the coach called my dad into his office. "Ziegler, you will be starting tonight at offensive guard and defensive tackle. I want you to play like you did the other day." My dad was elated. His time had arrived.

The game that night was a thriller, and my father made tackles all over the field. After one especially fierce hit late in the game, he was on the ground, slow to get up. His coach ran onto the field carrying something. My father was confused, thinking it was water. It turned out it was smelling salts. My dad shakily stood up and stayed in the game. During that era, there was no "concussion protocol." On the next play, an opposing player clipped him, breaking my father's lower leg. The football season was over for him.

Thanks to the two angels who appeared out of nowhere that afternoon and then disappeared into the dusk, my father became an excellent football player. His senior year, he played both ways on a competitive team. At the end of the season, Michigan State University offered him a full football scholarship.

My father was president of his high school senior class, though academically, he stood in the middle of the 500 plus students. At graduation, as class president, he sat in the front row, on stage facing the audience. As he listened to the accolades bestowed upon some of the top students, he looked out at the large crowd thinking most of the students graduating were average, just like him. To him, being average wasn't a detriment. My father had a strong conviction that his "average" classmates would be the ones who ended the war, established the peace, and rebuilt America.

The day after his graduation, my father, still seventeen years of age, boarded a train and moved to East Lansing to begin summer classes and football training at Michigan State University. He arrived on campus knowing no one. He signed up for a full summer schedule, and in addition to ROTC and football workouts, he was "up to his eyeballs" as he described it. Although he struggled and was homesick, he somehow made it through the summer session. He anxiously awaited the fall football season.

As a freshman, my father started at tight end and defensive tackle. His team played a packed schedule, traveling across the country, mostly by bus, and finished the 1945 season with a 5-3-1 record. The low point was a crushing loss to their arch-rival, the University of Michigan. But, according to him, there were some memorable moments. Against the University of Kentucky, which MSU won 7-6, my father played across from another 17-year-old, George Blanda, who would go on to become an NFL standout and Hall of Fame inductee. Against Pittsburgh, my father caught three passes including one for forty yards that set up the winning touchdown. After the game, a young kid waited for my dad to come out of the locker room. When he appeared, the kid scurried over, handed him a pen and program, and asked for his autograph. Surprised, my father stopped and signed the program. As he boarded the bus, my father expected heckling from his teammates, but they watched him, sitting silently in their seats. No one said a word. I guess they felt he deserved the honor that day. MSU lost to the University of Miami, a game played in Miami's historic old stadium, the Orange Bowl. My dad caught a pass on the goal line but couldn't score, and the tide of the game changed.

The morning after that game, my father awoke early, exited the El Commodore Hotel where the team was staying, and walked the streets of Miami. He was entranced by the tropical air and the palm fronds swaying in the ever-present Atlantic breeze. The memory of coconuts hanging from palm trees and fresh squeezed orange juice made before his eyes stayed with him as he boarded the team bus for the long trek back to the cold north. I suspect it was on the ride back to Michigan that he began plotting his eventual return to Florida.

The head football coach at MSU, Charlie Bachman, was another "angel" in my dad's life. My father adored him. Charlie, a former All-American who played for the legendary Knute Rockne at Notre Dame, had a respectable football pedigree. He was a "players' coach." My dad loved to tell me stories about him. In my young mind, "Coach" was almost a mythical figure.

My father turned eighteen during his freshman year of college, halfway through the football season. He had been in ROTC during high school continuing into college, and he and most of his peers assumed that they'd enlist or be drafted upon turning eighteen and handed the job of invading mainland Japan. From reports coming out of the islands, it was obvious that Japanese soldiers were brutal fighters, unwilling to give up even an inch of ground; that surrender without fighting to the death was not an option. It must have been a chilling proposition for an 18-year-old.

The atomic bomb changed all that, and the war ended shortly after my father's high school graduation, before he could legally enlist or be drafted into wartime service. His job, it turned out, would be keeping the peace and helping to rebuild Japan—kind of.

During the spring of his freshman year at MSU, he received a letter from the United States government telling him that the Selective Service had drafted him into the Army and to report to Cleveland for his physical. He could have sought a college deferment, and he considered doing so. He was conflicted. He had started on a solid division one football team and excelled as a freshman. His coaches told him he could be a major player, potentially All-American caliber. His conscience nagged, "You got lucky, but you still owe your country service." From the time of his "rebirth," he'd always assumed he'd be fighting this war. I suspect he spent a few sleepless nights stewing about his options.

Since he was in East Lansing, Michigan, he asked to have his physical performed in Detroit. When the morning came, he boarded a bus to Detroit. He felt alone, unsure of whether he was doing the right thing. Once he walked through the doors of the Army recruiting center and passed his Armed Forces physical examination, his destiny was cemented. My father experienced a sense of relief. He had made a decision, one that would alter the course of events in his life. It was time to leave football and college behind, at least temporarily. With some trepidation, he wondered what the future held in store.

After he finished the spring quarter at MSU, he returned to Cleveland to spend time with his family. In late March 1946, he received a letter of "Greetings from the President of the United States." The letter ordered him to report for duty on April 22nd.

In my mind, I can picture the day of his induction. My dad, tough, fearless, but also with a major soft side, eighteen years of age, waking up on a cold, probably gray, early spring morning, enjoying a quiet breakfast with his parents. The long walk from his cozy kitchen to his father's car. I picture his father, by this time in life worn down physically, starting to lose his vitality from working long hours, raising a family through the Depression under constant financial pressure, worsened by the cumulative damage of bad habits. I imagine my grandfather slowly descending the rickety stairs of their old double decker, heavy-hearted at the prospect of sending his young, handsome son into the unknown. The two of them sitting in the car, silent, driving down the early morning streets of Cleveland, both wishing the ride didn't have to end. The car pulling up in front of the Army recruiting center, stopping, and both doors opening. My dad reaching into the back seat to grab his bag as his father slowly walked around the front of the car. Their eyes locking briefly. Sadness tempered by an underlying feeling of excitement in my father and by pride in his father. A quick hug, and then my dad watching his father slowly get back into the car and drive away.

My father ended up stationed at Fort Knox near Louisville, Kentucky for basic training, assigned to artillery, transporting and firing 105 Howitzers. At the end of basic training, he awaited orders,

29

hoping for assignment to Europe where he could practice and perfect his German. Instead, he received notice that he would be heading west, to Japan. My dad was disappointed, but he was granted a long furlough, several weeks to go home and relax before deploying. He boarded a bus, headed back to Cleveland, and settled into civilian life. The Army extended his furlough twice, turning it into a prolonged leave, and it wasn't until eight weeks later that he received notice to report to Camp Stoneman, located on San Francisco Bay.

A few days before flying out to report for duty, my father learned that there was an Army football league at Boiling Field near Washington, D.C. He obtained a phone number and spoke with a Colonel at the base who became attentive when he heard my dad had played at MSU. He said he would need to verify this, for my dad to stay by the phone, and that he would call him back in thirty minutes. When the Colonel called back, he was even more excited, except that there was one big problem. Boiling Field was Army Air Corp and my dad was a rookie draftee in the Army. So began a flurry of phone calls up the order of rank, possibly all the way to the Secretary of War. At the end of the day, the Colonel contacted my dad. Those in charge decided it would set a bad precedent to transfer an unseasoned Army draftee into the Air Corp just to play football. This news dashed my father's high hopes, and "with a lump in his throat and a heavy feeling in his heart," he wondered what lay ahead in Japan. A few days later, he boarded a DC-3 and flew to San Francisco.

He arrived in California mid-morning and did not have to report to Camp Stoneman until late in the evening. He wandered around San Francisco, walking its hills, and ended up on the bayfront looking out at Alcatraz. Soldiers and sailors packed the streets, heading to or returning from occupied territories. He knew no one and felt alone in the big city. He caught an early movie. At the movie, he ran into jazz great, Duke Ellington. After the movie, he grew weary of being alone in a strange city. He checked into Camp Stoneman early.

A few days later he walked through a portal that proclaimed, "Through this arch pass the best damn troops in the world." He boarded a ferry and slowly chugged across San Francisco Bay to his transport vessel. As he neared the shipping terminal, he saw a sleek, gray troop ship tethered to the dock. He could make out its name, the "Rensselaer Victory."

Victory ships were mass produced, armed cargo ships. Some were reconfigured to move troops. Japan had decimated America's Pacific fleet at Pearl Harbor four years earlier. Immediately after that devastating blow, President Roosevelt forced the previously sleeping American industrial-military complex into high gear. The building and equipping of its naval fleet to fight a war on two fronts was possibly the most impressive feat of the war effort.

Anticipating an eventual invasion of mainland Japan, the United States would need to move a massive number of troops across the Pacific. Victory ships, with a length of 455 feet, a beam of 62 feet, and a cruising speed of seventeen knots, much faster than their predecessor, the Liberty ships, fit the bill. They could outrun German U-boats and transport over 1,500 men per vessel. In less than two years, shipyards built over 550 of these ships employing novel mass production techniques including the use of prefabricated sections. Sadly, these boats are now almost extinct with only three remaining, the Rensselaer not one of them.

My father disembarked from the ferry and joined a crowd of 1,400 soldiers on the dock. A sergeant with a bullhorn called his name, and he boarded the transport ship over the single gangway. A Petty Officer directed him down into the ship's hold. Inside, he found canvas bunks strapped between iron poles stacked four or five high. My father was assigned a prized second tier bunk, easier to access and more stable than the upper ones. After stowing his gear, he climbed back topside, and after all were aboard, the ship set off.

James W. Ziegler, M.D.

The views were breathtaking in all directions, and the sight of the setting sun to the west and the twinkling lights of traffic crossing the Golden Gate Bridge behind him were mesmerizing. The rugged coastline of Northern California soon faded into the distance.

All went well for a day or two, but as the rolling of the boat from side to side increased on the open ocean, seasickness set in. Everyone was throwing up. The lavatories, the galley, and the ship's topside were a mess, covered with vomit. A single cable at the edge of the ship's deck was the only thing that separated soldiers and crew from a fall into the water below. Soldiers held on for dear life as they vomited over the side of the ship. As they became weaker, most soldiers stayed in their bunks, unable to eat or drink, moaning in agony. And just when they thought they were all going to die, the seasickness subsided. Normalcy returned.

The next fourteen days passed without incident. The ship inched toward Japan, and on the 21st day after leaving California, it pulled into Yokohama Bay. At the entrance to the harbor, a huge Japanese warship lay on its side. Opposite the partially submerged, war-beaten vessel was a break wall where American GIs had painted on the rocks "Kilroy was here." Once in the protected harbor, heavy ropes secured my father's ship to an extensive unloading dock.

My father and the other soldiers remained on deck for some time as Japanese workers scurried about below and unloaded cargo from the ship's hold. While playing hearts with some of his new friends, my dad noticed part of a newspaper wedged under a lifeboat a few feet away. He walked over, grabbed and un-crumpled it. For the first time in his life, he read the *Stars and Stripes,* the official Army newspaper. His eyes caught a caption at the bottom of an inside page: "the 8th Army football team begins practice at Keio University in a week." He hadn't thought about football since the Boiling Fields disappointment, but a plan took shape in his mind. He now knew how he was going to spend his time in Japan, though he had no idea how he was going to make it happen.

Road Worthy

The soldiers finally disembarked from the Victory ship, loaded onto trucks, and were transported to the train station. A train took them twenty miles north of Yokohama to the 4th Replacement Depot, also known as Camp Zama. Prior to World War II, the site housed the Imperial Japanese Army Academy, the West Point equivalent of Japanese Army officer training. After the war, it became a United States Army post, a sprawling tent city through which every US soldier entered and left Japan. An orderly assigned my father to a cot in one of the thousands of tents.

It felt good to be on solid ground after three weeks of swaying at sea, and my father reported for evening chow and then went back to his tent, stashed his gear, and fell asleep. At dawn, he was awakened by a Military Policeman standing outside his tent impatiently shouting his name.

"Ziegler, get dressed and follow me."

The command unnerved my father. He wondered what he had done wrong. When my father emerged from his tent, the MP took off at a brisk walk, and my father followed.

The MP led him to the Provost Marshall's office, directed him into a back room, and told him to sit and wait. The door closed, and my father sat in an uncomfortable chair, alone with his thoughts. He'd had some minor run-ins with superior officers during basic training. He'd also almost been caught stealing a fresh loaf of bread from the Victory Ship's kitchen one evening to share with his hungry bunkmates. Were these past actions finally catching up with him?

The door opened, and the MP shepherded two other privates into the small room. The door closed again, leaving the three men staring at one another. A shared feeling of uneasiness prevailed, but nobody spoke. After ten minutes or so, a captain entered the room.

Sensing the mounting anxiety of the three men and clearly enjoying it, the captain glared at them, and asked, "Men, do you know why you are here?"

After a long silence, the captain smiled and said, "Each of you had a year of ROTC in college. I would like you to stay here at the depot and become military policemen"

The three men let out a collective sigh of relief. The first two men signed on instantly. My father was reluctant. He told the captain that he didn't think he'd make a good MP.

The captain walked up to my father, clearly agitated, and stared him down, "Soldier, let me tell you about the other 1400 troops that arrived here with you. They are going to Southern Japan. They will be eating K rations, living in pup tents, training in the field with live ammo. Are you sure you want to go with them?"

My father knew that Camp Zama was thirty miles from To-kyo, the home of Keio University, training site of the 8th Army foot-ball team. Going south would take him further away and lessen his chance of connecting with the team.

He replied, "Captain. Sir. Is this part of the 8th Army?"

The captain replied, "Hell yes, toughest unit in our grand na-tion's Army."

My father said, "Well then, Sir, I'd like to stay here."

Without any training, my father was issued a white helmet liner, arm bands with MP on them, and a .45-caliber pistol. He tried to get information about the 8th Army football team, but no one at the Depot knew much. As soon as he had a day off, he took a train into Yokohama, found Special Services, and told an officer he'd like to join the 8th Army football team. The Special Services officer pe-rused my dad's records and told him to go back to the Depot. He would pass my father's information on to the coaches in Tokyo.

My father hated life as an MP. He didn't like his partner or the sergeant in charge. Both had Japanese girls "on the side," and both were stealing items from the Army and selling them on the black market. He felt he was on a collision course with the two men. Thankfully, his order for transfer to the 8th Army football team at Keio University came through within a few days.

Keio University was located a few miles south of central To-kyo and about twenty miles north of Yokohama. The university housed the 8th Army football team in one of the dormitories on its elegant, historic campus. After finding the college, my father wandered among the Japanese students and eventually made his way to the Army football team's dorm. He checked in and was assigned a room with two other players. Compared to his earlier Army digs, the accommodations were plush.

There were several other Division One college football play-ers, a few from teams my father had competed against during his freshman year at MSU. Since there were several tight ends among the group, my father established himself as a tackle. Everyone was excited to be there, and the connection among the players was im-mediate.

For the next four months, my father's life centered around football. He was in a foreign country, thousands of miles from home, but the focal point of his existence was little changed. The two coaches, a captain and a lieutenant, held rank over the players, but they knew very little about running a team. They composed a play-book and handed it out to the players at evening mess. My father, having quickly assessed the talents of his teammates, realized that most of the coaches' plays did not take advantage of the players' strengths. He changed several plays, threw out others, and created new ones. The team gave the revised playbook back to the coaches the next morning. The coaches seemed relieved and never said any-thing.

Practice took up most of the morning. The rest of the day was unstructured. My dad developed a close-knit group of friends including the team manager, whose name was Ralph. Ralph was the "Brother Rat" of the group. He could get his hands on anything. A few weeks after the team's assemblage, he showed up one afternoon with a small Army truck. My dad's closest friends now had wheels, and they soon discovered that between the two movie theaters in

Tokyo and the one in Yokohama, they could catch a show almost every night. For the next three months, my father's group never lacked for nighttime entertainment.

Ralph had a knack for navigating, and he quickly figured out all the roads between Keio University, Tokyo, and Yokohama. My dad described memories of flying through rice paddies after late shows, in total darkness in the middle of nowhere, and Ralph always safely getting them home.

The Army football league consisted of seven teams with games every Sunday afternoon. The seven teams played each other twice over the course of the season. Usually, large, rowdy crowds of soldiers and sailors attended the games. My father ran into several guys he knew from stateside. He also had a few interesting interactions on the field.

Against the 24th division, he played on the defensive line. The opposing offensive tackle kept holding him. After a few plays, my father looked over at the line official and yelled, "This guy's holding me. Are you blind?"

The official ran over to my father, grabbed his shoulder pads, and barely able to restrain himself, spat out, "Soldier, under this striped shirt, is a colonel. One more peep out of you, and you are out of this game, and that may not be all." Needless to say, my father received a quick lesson on the reach of Army politics. He complained no more.

During the two games against First Cavalry, my father had run-ins with one tight end with the first name Rebel. Rebel had played for the University of Alabama's Crimson Tide, and he was fresh off an appearance in the Rose Bowl. Based on his football credentials, he was a little cocky, a "prima donna" as my father described him. Years later, when I was in college, I took my new, very shy college girlfriend, who was from Birmingham, Alabama, to Florida for Spring Break. She stayed with friends but came over one night to visit my family and have dinner. When my father sat down at the dinner table, he looked at her and in a disgusted tone said, "I only know one person from Birmingham, Alabama, and he has the ridiculous first name Rebel."

My girlfriend Kathy replied, "His last name isn't Steiner, is it?"

Incredulous, my father asked, "You know him?"

Kathy, now clearly uncomfortable, replied, "He's my neighbor. And one of my father's friends."

My dad, never one to mince his words said, "Well tell him I said the Big Ten will always be better than the Southeastern Conference."

With that, he excused himself from dinner and plopped down in front of the television.

During my father's time in Japan, one opposing team, the 24th Division, was based in Kokura on the island of Kyushu. Kokura was an industrial city, strategically very important during the war because of its arms factories and vast stores of munitions. When the US government and its allies decided to drop the atom bomb, officials picked Kokura as the secondary target for the first bomb and the primary target for the second. Briefing officers told the pilots to only release the bombs if they had direct vision of their immediate targets. The first mission went off without problems, with the bomber Enola Gay dropping a uranium bomb over central Hiroshima. Three days later, a B-29 carrying a hydrogen bomb, much more powerful than the first bomb, lifted off from Tinian in the Mariana Islands with the intention of dropping the bomb on a large munitions factory in central Kokura. Early that day, the sky was clear over Kokura. However, as the B-29 approached, transient cloud cover floated in. The pilot did three flyovers, but he couldn't get a direct visual on the factory that was the central target. After the third pass, the plane flew on to Nagasaki. Kokura—the "luckiest city in Japan"—was spared.

James W. Ziegler, M.D.

The 8th Army played the 24th Division in Kokura on Thanksgiving Day. My father's team took an overnight train ride from Tokyo. The players tried to sleep in berths designed for the average Japanese. Half their bodies stuck out into the aisles, and nobody got much sleep.

At dusk, the train passed through Hiroshima. The soldiers were silent as they looked out on utter devastation stretching as far as the eye could see. They found it hard to imagine the impact of the two atomic bombs, between 50,000 and 100,000 casualties, instantly and without warning. Even before dropping the atomic bombs, the Allies had carried out a conventional firebombing campaign that had destroyed most major Japanese cities, including sixteen square miles in central Tokyo. But the scene in Hiroshima was far worse, unlike anything any of them had ever seen.

I'm sure my father, along with other American soldiers, was aware of the millions of homeless, starving Japanese citizens. Their faces stared blankly, showing no emotion—victims of the imperial government's militaristic and nationalistic indoctrination. Hundreds of thousands of orphans roamed city streets, and my father's team adopted one young teenager and took care of him during their stay at Keio University. The young teen had been in training to become a Kamikaze pilot prior to the war's ending.

My dad didn't say much about the game in Kokura. He did, however, relay great memories of the Thanksgiving dinner served afterwards, partly because it included all the traditional fixings from home but also because the soldiers felt so fortunate to be alive and healthy, free from the despondency that surrounded them.

My father's team completed the regular season in second place. As a reward, the league sent the players to Kawana, a scenic resort with a golf course, pools, and hot springs. They stayed for a week. Upon returning to Keio University, my father learned that he'd made the Japan US Armed Forces all-star team. This team played an all-star team from Korea a few weeks later and won 13-0.

The league again rewarded my father and his teammates with a week at a resort hotel where he soaked in hot springs and enjoyed luxurious accommodations and fine dining. After the week ended, his football career in the Army was over.

Within a week, the players received orders to report to Special Services in Yokohama to receive new assignments. My father and his close group of friends packed up their gear, and Ralph picked them up in the truck. They drove in silence to Yokohama, appreciative of the time they had spent together but wondering what lie ahead. They knew the draft had ended in the United States so no soldiers would replace them. They had no idea how long their tours would last.

Ralph parked the truck at the Special Services complex. The soldiers went inside. My father did not want to return to the Depot or resume duty as an MP. He asked if there were any other posts available. He was relieved to hear that Fryer Gym, the main recreational facility for the 8th Army, needed someone to supervise the recreation and sports programs. My father volunteered for the position.

His teammates received assignments throughout Japan. Before the group broke up, they met in the lobby of the Special Services building. As they descended the steps outside, they noticed two MPs walking around their truck, recording its license and other details. My father and his teammates shook hands and said their goodbyes. As they walked by the truck, each man rubbed its fender or kicked its tires, avoiding eye contact with the two MPs. They made their way to the train station and then split up to go their separate ways. The MPs transported the truck back to its rightful owner, the United States Army.

My father's new job was with the 12th Special Services Company, overseen by a Captain who really liked him. The Captain tried to convince my father to join the regular Army and attend

Officer Candidate School. My father was not interested in making the Army a career.

The 12th Special Services Company ran golf courses, movie theaters, the gym, and other recreational activities for GIs who had earned leave time. A Japanese carpenter built a little room for my dad under the bleachers, so for the next two months, he lived in a makeshift plywood room. A typical day started out with donuts and coffee at the Red Cross Building and a leisurely perusal of *Stars and Stripes* from cover to cover. He then supervised basketball games, golf tournaments, and other recreational events. On one occasion, he acted as an official for an ice-skating tournament, a sport I'm sure he knew nothing about. In the evening, my father sometimes took trains into Yokohama or Tokyo. He described the massive destruction in these cities.

In early March 1947, my father received word that his tour of duty was ending. The US Army in Japan was demobilizing. He reported to Yokohama, and a few days later boarded the troop ship, General Langfitt, for his voyage back to the United States.

As his ship pulled out of Yokohama Harbor, my father thought back over the previous nine months. He had left for Japan feeling fearful, uncertain, and reluctant. He returned to the States feeling thankful. He had made several great friends, "average" guys just like him, men who would go on to do important things and remain friends for life. He had seen the aftermath of war's horror, though he never had to stare down the enemy, and he rarely had to carry a loaded weapon. He observed and experienced a different culture, and he watched with awe the resiliency of the Japanese people as they recovered and rebuilt. All that, and he didn't miss a football season! He was filled with appreciation and optimism as the troop ship slowly made its way across the Pacific.

The return trip was quicker than the outgoing, and after two weeks at sea his ship pulled into San Francisco Bay. My father was overwhelmed with joy as the ship passed under the Golden Gate

Bridge. He saw the lights of San Francisco sparkling in the near distance. After disembarking, he returned to Camp Stoneman and passed again under the arch that proclaimed on its reverse, "Through this portal return the best damn soldiers in the world." It took a few weeks to complete his discharge from the Army, but soon he was a civilian, on a train speeding eastward.

My father had maintained no contact with Michigan State University during his year in the Army. When he arrived back in Cleveland, he heard that MSU had replaced Coach Bachman with a new head coach. My father reported to MSU the day after he returned home, and the new coach made it clear that my father was not part of the future plan for the MSU football program. He had brought in new recruits, intent on completely changing and rejuvenating things. My father had two choices. He could keep his guaranteed scholarship and suffer demotion to the scrubs, or he could leave. He chose the latter.

He enrolled at Baldwin Wallace, a small liberal arts college in the Cleveland suburb of Berea. The GI Bill paid his tuition, and he lived at home, commuting each morning from downtown Cleveland. Though disappointed by the reception he'd received at MSU, my dad quickly made new friends at BW, and it turned out that the football team there was very competitive, with a few players who would go on to compete in the NFL. He settled in.

One day in the early fall of his senior year, he walked by the college tennis courts. He noticed two coeds playing, and he stopped to watch, enthralled by their laughter and carefree demeanor. As he got closer, he recognized the player on the far side of the court, Joan Nichol, a girl he'd had a wicked crush on in middle school—a real "knock out" as he described her. They were in the same grade, but she attended a different high school.

As a teen, my father occasionally saw her at the Puritas Springs Roller Rink in Cleveland. Afraid of rejection, he often admired her from a distance, but he never worked up the nerve to talk

41

to her. The other tennis player's name was Alice, and my father had a class with her. He walked away plotting. A few days later he approached Alice in class.

"Alice, do you think you could put in a good word for me with Joan?"

Alice, who had characterized my dad as an egotistical jock, replied, "Absolutely not. You are a jerk!"

My father was devastated, but he continued scheming. When one of his football teammates began dating a sorority sister of Joan's, my dad asked his friend if his girlfriend would fix my father up with Joan on a double date. His friend's girlfriend agreed.

That weekend, the four of them went to a Cleveland Orchestra Pops Concert at Public Hall in downtown Cleveland. My father tried to "play it cool," but Joan's beauty and sophistication overwhelmed him. Tongue-tied, he fumbled over his words. Joan smiled as he tried to make awkward conversation. He finally asked her if she remembered him from middle or high school. Joan replied that she remembered him as a guy who never shaved and always needed a haircut. My father took this as a huge compliment. At least she had noticed him. There was hope.

They began dating, and a few months later my father's entire fraternity marched down to her sorority house. They stood outside her window, arms draped over one another, singing sentimental songs. At the end of this choral barrage, my father offered Joan his fraternity pin. She accepted; they were officially college sweethearts.

Despite her lack of interest in football, Joan dutifully began attending my father's games. He played especially well against Mount Union College, whose star was their fullback, Napoleon Bell, a former teammate of my dad's on the 8th Army football team in Japan. Napoleon was a fierce competitor, and my father really admired him.

My dad played both ways that night. Hard fought from beginning to end, BW won the game. Afterwards, my father, bruised and battered but sure that he'd impressed Joan, asked her what she thought of the game.

She replied, "Well it was quite good, I think."

He said, "Do you remember when I nailed the quarterback?"

She replied, "Well actually, no, but it was a very exciting game."

He continued, "Do you remember when I stopped the end-around run and tackled the ball carrier to stop their final drive?"

She replied, "Well no. Did you really do that?"

Frustrated by his obvious failure to impress her, he asked, "Did you see any part of the game?"

She said, "Well I did spend a lot of time talking to the girls, and I wasn't really sure what your number was."

My father realized he was going to have to find other ways to win her admiration.

Joan graduated with a math major a semester earlier than my dad. She began working for NASA as a "human computer" while my father completed his final semester. He had started college intent on becoming a dentist, but the coursework proved overwhelming, and he had not done well in the introductory math and science classes. He then gravitated toward education with a minor in PE, thinking he, like most ex-jocks, would end up coaching.

During his last year at Baldwin Wallace, my father was assigned to Fairview High School in a suburb of Cleveland to complete his student teaching. His supervisor there knew that he played football at BW. The football team at Fairview High was struggling. On the first day of student teaching, my father was asked to help a small group of players improve their line play. For an hour every day he worked with this group of kids and loved it. They were motivated, willing to work hard, and intent on improving. My father felt like he was paying forward what the two angels had done for him.

My parents got married in the spring, a little over a year following my father's December graduation. The ceremony was simple, held in the BW College Chapel. My father's best man was his sister Betty's husband, Bill Opperman. As my father stood in the back of the chapel with my Uncle Bill, he gazed out the small windows. He watched guys playing basketball in the back of his old fraternity house and experienced the pre-marriage jitters. He then moved to the front of the chapel. As he stood at the altar and watched his bride walk down the aisle, all doubts vanished. He wondered how the kid from 84th Street had wooed such a classy woman.

A few years after getting married, with help from my mom's mother, my parents bought an old farmhouse on twenty acres of land in Olmsted Falls, a small town outside Cleveland. Behind the house were an immense barn and a smaller chicken coop that then led through an orchard to open fields. After my older sister Ellen was born, my mother quit working. My father held various jobs, including teaching, coaching, and a three-year stint as a salesman. The old farmhouse and outbuildings needed major renovations, and my father did most of the repairs himself. He was constantly working-- fixing and adding onto the house, building stalls in the barn, cutting trails through the fields, putting in gardens, and planting trees and flowers.

As a kid who had grown up on a forty-foot city lot, my father stood in awe of his wide expanse of land. On summer evenings, he loved throwing one of his five children onto his shoulders and hiking the perimeter of the twenty acres. One of my earliest memories is walking out the back door of our house with my parents and my dad grabbing me and throwing me onto his shoulders. From my high vantage point, I slowly watched the world go by as my parents walked, hand in hand, past the big red barn, through the orchard, and around the trails of their country "estate." As I held onto my father's head, I felt like a king.

Somehow my parents, mostly my father I think, thought that since they owned a farm, they should make it look and feel like one. Soon our family of seven acquired horses, chickens, bunnies, dogs, and cats. The barn had a huge haymow packed with bales of hay and straw. My older sisters, Ellen and Evie, and I cared for the horses. We cleaned out their stalls, fed them, and made sure they always had water.

Since our neighbors had large adjoining fields, we grew up riding horses as our primary mode of transportation. We had hundreds of acres at our disposal. It was idyllic, and I think my parents experienced great satisfaction exposing us to open space and nature's beauty, a contrast to their upbringing in the noisy, crowded city.

After teaching, coaching, a few stints in industry, and with a wife and four kids (my brother Joe was not yet born) and a twenty-acre farm that needed constant attention, my father decided that he wanted to be his own boss. He applied to and was accepted by Cleveland Marshall Law School. He worked full days and then took evening classes, arriving home each night long after the rest of our family was asleep. His schedule was grueling and pushed my dad to his limit. During his final year, he was short on funds and unable to pay the tuition. He went to the Dean of the law school, Wilson G. Stapleton, and asked if he could defer payment for the upcoming term. Dean Stapleton turned out to be another angel in my father's life. He pulled my dad's file, noted his service in the Army, and after a quick perusal of his record, told him to sign up for classes and not to worry about paying.

After graduating from law school, my father continued to teach and coach, practicing law part time with my mother as his secretary. He converted the front part of our old farmhouse into a law office with a small reception area. He also built a carwash next to our house on the frontage facing the road. Three years later, he gave up teaching and coaching for good to practice law and manage the carwash.

When I was in third grade, my father decided to buy a huge, run-down nine-bedroom Victorian "cottage" on a quiet island in the western basin of Lake Erie. It was about an hour's drive plus a forty-minute ferry boat ride from our farm. Between late June and late August, we spent every weekend at our island retreat. Of course, as we were all running about, playing, swimming, boating, skiing, and causing all kinds of mischief, my dad worked.

My sister Ellen described my father's summer days of vacation best. "*Shortly after breakfast, my dad walks out the front door carrying a hammer. He is hunting for the screen door that was banging the night before. Since it is still early in the morning, he has not yet begun to sweat, but by mid-morning, a rivulet of sweat will begin dripping off his nose as he pulls rotting wood off the porch floor, and it will continue when he's fixing and replacing the window. It will drip when he is pulling the starter rope on the rusty old lawn mower, and he will still be sweating while painting the kitchen cabinets as the sun is setting.*"

When I finished fifth grade, my dad decided to buy a large German chalet in town, closer to where we went to school. The owner had scheduled the house for demolition, but my father had a vision of restoring it to its earlier splendor. He kept his law practice in the front of the old farmhouse, which was only a few miles away, continued to run the car wash, and rented out the back of the farmhouse to tenants. He also leased the fields to a lima bean grower. He was now overseeing a family of seven, running two businesses, and maintaining three old homes. To add to the craziness, a foreign exchange student from Norway became good friends with my sister Ellen and confided to her that she was miserable living with her assigned family. Over dinner one night, Ellen asked my father if her new Norwegian friend, Tove, could move in with us.

My father said, "I don't know if this is a great time."

My mother said, "Of course she can."

I had missed the dinner conversation. Nobody told me I had a new sister. After four days of waking up every morning and seeing Tove in our kitchen eating breakfast, I asked Ellen if her redhaired friend was ever going home. It was then my parents told me that Tove was now a part of our family. She blended perfectly into the craziness of the Ziegler household.

Over Christmas break during my middle school years, my father packed the entire family into our *Volkswagon* van and drove for 24 straight hours to South Florida. The first two trips we stayed with friends and acquaintances. The third trip we rented a small house right across the street from the ocean in Deerfield Beach. Our good friends, the Hecker family, rented a house a few doors down, and for one week we enjoyed the South Florida sun and warm ocean breeze.

Every morning, my father sat in a lounge chair just outside the front door of our rental, a big glass of fresh orange juice next to him, his eyes closed and a dreamy look on his face. It was the perfect family vacation—exceptional weather, unstructured togetherness, and an abundance of smiles and laughs. We were all sad to leave for the long ride back to Ohio.

For three years, my father had flirted with the idea of moving the family to Florida. He was done with the long, cold, gray Ohio winters. The brief stay in Deerfield Beach cemented our destiny.

Unbeknownst to me and my siblings, my parents had spent one afternoon during our vacation looking at houses in Deerfield Beach. When we returned to Ohio, with my mother's unenthusiastic endorsement, my father called the owner of the house my mother liked the most and made an offer. The owners accepted.

My mother was devastated. She sobbed at night when alone with my father, inwardly terrified of such a huge change. My dad had no reservations, no worries about the uncertain future. He was intent on selling off all his Ohio assets, completely cutting the cord from his earlier life, taking the Florida Bar, packing up his family of kids ranging from eight to nineteen years of age, and starting anew on Florida's Gold Coast. His only concern arose from a recurring nightmare. In his dream, he pulls into the Florida Welcome Station. We emerge from the VW van, stretch our cramped legs, and as we are piling back in to continue southward, the supervisor of the Welcome Station runs toward us yelling, "There's no more room. You will have to go back to Ohio."

Eight months later, we moved to Florida. We blew past the Florida Welcome Station and continued down the Florida Turnpike, not getting off until we hit the exit near Deerfield Beach. It was early 'August with oppressive heat, ninety degrees every day with 100% humidity. Initially nobody, including my mother, was happy. We were crammed into a small Florida home, torn away from our very comfortable and contented lives in Ohio. We knew no one.

I sometimes wonder why my father decided at the age of 45 to pick up and make such a drastic change. In Ohio, we had a comfortable home and an idyllic summer existence. As a family, we were connected to the pulse of our little Ohio town. We all thrived, each in a different way.

I think there were probably several reasons. My father clearly hated winter. With Ellen in college and my older sister Evie and me in our teenage years, I wonder if he felt like I did when my oldest daughter Meg left for college—that his kids were growing up too fast, exerting too much independence, and slipping away. Could it have been a last-ditch effort to pull us back, to cheat time and recreate the family togetherness we'd experienced when younger and on our last trip to Florida? Did he think life would be easier and the opportunities greater? Or was he motivated by his own selfish desire to live in what he considered paradise?

Whatever my father's reasons, which he never shared with any of us, I have to give him credit. He certainly had conviction. He had no job, little savings, and no comprehensive plan. He hadn't even begun studying for the Florida Bar that he would have to pass in order to practice law in Florida. And he had five miserable kids and an unhappy wife. The stakes were high.

CHAPTER 3
The Mallet Resurfaces

S hortly after acquiring the mallet, my father thoroughly cleaned it and discovered engraved letters on the opposite side of the "Andersonville, GA" inscription. Once the grime was removed, he could read the initials JKP (at the time he thought JRP) and the last name Ferrell. Under the name was a town—Uhrichsville, Ohio. Since he had traveled throughout Ohio playing football in college, my father was familiar with the town.

After cleaning the mallet, I suspect my father periodically wondered about JKP Ferrell from Uhrichsville, Ohio. But, after the initial excitement of finding the mysterious item receded, he mostly went about his life and forgot about the mallet. Through the rest of high school and during breaks home from college, I remember seeing the mallet in various places in our home—on my parents' big white dresser, on a shelf in our den, on the mantle over the fireplace in our family room. And then it seemed to disappear.

In 1978, a few years after discovering the mallet, my parents attended my sister Evie's college graduation in Wooster, Ohio. On the long drive back to Florida, they visited Uhrichsville and spent one afternoon walking around the two cemeteries in town hunting for the tombstone of JKP Ferrell. They never found it. The puzzle remained unsolved, and my father moved on to other pressing matters. I don't recall him ever mentioning the mallet in conversation as the years went by.

Over the next twenty years, I finished college in Atlanta, Georgia, attended medical school at the University of Florida, and completed a pediatric residency in Tampa, Florida. After residency, I worked for one year in Melbourne, Florida. During those years I was passionate about the Florida outdoors, especially the Keys, where my parents had purchased a second home. I had a fifteen-foot classic Boston Whaler powered by a seventy horsepower Evinrude outboard. Any time I wasn't working, I was fishing, snorkeling, or exploring. I loved the Florida ocean, and I especially enjoyed being in or on the water with my brother Joe and my brother-in-law Arlan.

When I moved to Melbourne to work as a general Pediatrician, I rented a condo on a long stretch of mostly deserted beach south of town. I surf-fished almost every day, and my refrigerator and freezer were always filled with fresh fish caught just over the dune directly in front of my unit. My brother Joe was still in college in Gainesville about two hours away, and he visited me on the beach any weekend his schedule allowed. The two of us fished together all day and frequently long into the night.

I accepted a fellowship at Massachusetts General Hospital in pediatric critical care medicine halfway through my year in Melbourne. I planned to sojourn north for two years of subspecialty training and then return to my beloved Florida. The hospital in Melbourne even offered to build a small pediatric intensive care unit for me upon my return.

At the end of my year in Melbourne, my friends threw a going away party for me. My brother drove over for it. Toward the end of the day, I was standing outside with him on the raised deck of my condominium. We were cooking fish on the grill, looking westward at the sun setting over the orange groves lining the east bank of the Indian River.

Joe grabbed my arm. With a sad, and, for him, unusually serious look, he locked eyes with me and said, "Dude, you are never coming back."

"What do you mean?" I asked.

He replied, "You are going to meet some woman, and you will not come back to Florida."

I thought he was crazy, and I said it. "You're insane man. There's no way I'm not coming back home."

At the end of June, I relocated to Boston. My brother was right. After my year living on the beach in Melbourne, I moved on to adulthood. I finished my fellowship, met my future wife Joy, got married, moved to Denver to pursue further training in pediatric cardiology, and eventually landed in Rhode Island where Joy and I raised our two daughters. I never again lived in Florida.

As my life became more chaotic with years of additional subspecialty training followed by my move to Rhode Island, a demanding, time-consuming job, and family commitments, my dad's life slowed down. He closed his law practice, and my parents sold our large family home in Deerfield Beach and moved to a smaller house in Boca Raton, one town north. At the age of sixty, they bought a vacation home in Redstone, Colorado, a tiny hamlet in the Crystal River Valley, just over the mountains from Aspen. They began spending May through October in Colorado. After their first few years there, my sister Edie and her husband Gary bought a small house in Redstone, settled in, grew a business, and raised their family. My other siblings and I always included a week in Colorado as part of our summertime vacations, sometimes all converging there at the same time for hiking, mountain biking, camping, and exploring.

In his mid-sixties, my dad began to manifest unremitting signs of central nervous system dysfunction. First, a mild left sided weakness that had plagued him since his forties gradually worsened. His equilibrium faltered, and he started walking with a swaying gait; at times, he needed to grab onto something (or someone) to keep from falling. He then developed features of Parkinson's with the onset of an intention tremor and loss of fine motor skills. In his seventies, on top of everything else, he developed autonomic dysfunction characterized by abrupt and uncomfortable changes in heart rate and blood pressure, dizziness, and urinary urgency.

Despite the limitations imposed by aging, my father, at times, refused to acknowledge and surrender to his declining health. Things came to a head in his late sixties on a summer day in Colorado. As my sister Edie was trying to start my parents' old lawn mower, my father looked on. After several unsuccessful attempts, my dad limped over, nudged her aside, and determinedly bent down and grabbed the starter rope. Before Edie could stop him, he yanked upward, lost his balance, and flew back into a patch of overgrown weeds and brambles, landing on his back. He was unable to right himself. Noting the defeated and pleading look on his face, my sister was heartbroken as she hurried over to assist him. She summoned her husband Gary for help, and the two of them extricated my dad, pulled him upright, and carefully supported him into the house. My dad remained silent, as if ashamed of his broken state and inability to perform what previously would have been the simplest of tasks. He was never the same after that, his self-confidence and pride broken by infirmity.

As his symptoms became more debilitating, my dad grew anxious and then depressed. He saw several specialists. A neurologist diagnosed him with Parkinson's disease and started him on medications, which temporarily slowed progression of some of his symptoms. In his seventies, my father saw a new subspecialist who diagnosed him with multiple system atrophy, a progressive, fatal, degenerative disease of the brain of unclear cause, though some have speculated previous, repetitive head trauma as an inciting precursor. I am sure my father sustained several concussions during sandlot sports, street fights, and his football days. I suspect that the cumulative damage eventually caught up with him.

With time, my father became less social, more anxious, and mostly housebound. Thankfully, his cognitive function and acute senses were spared. He remained in complete control of his thought processes, as quick-witted as he had been decades earlier when arguing a case before a judge. He could also hear a pin drop from across the room.

My dad turned 76 on October 31, 2003. His health had insidiously worsened, and he was having a harder time navigating usual activities of daily living. In some ways, his compromised state weighed more heavily on him because of my mom's exceptionally good health and boundless energy. He did not want to burden her or steal any of her endless vitality. Each morning, with the aid of a walker, he lumbered into the kitchen, took his medications, ate fresh Florida fruit, and sat and completed the morning crossword puzzle with my mother. He occasionally maneuvered onto his three-wheel bike and pedaled around the neighborhood. He had not lost his passion for exploring, and sometimes he would sneak over to a nearby thrift shop's dumpster to look for special "finds."

Nighttime was especially difficult for him. He could not fall asleep and often sat alone for hours trying to shut his brain down and drift off. In his final years, he could not make peace with the night. I think he also experienced moments of panic. My sister Ellen lived nearby and was a shining angel of support, often massaging his shoulders for hours, offering reassurance. I suspect he realized how fortunate he was, and I'm sure Ellen's presence gave him great solace. Still, he knew that his health would continue to deteriorate and that he was helpless to stop it. It was exceptionally daunting for such a self-made, independent person, now unable to control his daily existence or his destiny.

One cool December evening in 2003, my father walked into the back-storage room of his house, a dark and musty place where most of my parents' junk had accumulated. Eyeing the many shelves that lined the walls, he spotted the mallet covered with a thick layer of dust. He picked it up and carried it out to the kitchen. He cleaned it off and sat at the kitchen table, rotating it in his hands as he stared down at it.

For a moment, my dad forgot his age. He didn't care that he was home alone. He wondered again about JKP Ferrell and why this mallet had ended up in his hands. He pictured a Union soldier in the wilderness enduring the rigors of war and the horrors of Andersonville. In some ways, at some moments, my dad's life had become a living hell. This poor Civil War soldier had gone through much worse. My dad connected with him; he realized he needed to discover the mallet's origin. The mallet became an obsession. It gave my father a renewed interest in living. It made him acknowledge that life is a gift given by God to every human being, not always perfect or easy, but a precious gift, nonetheless.

As he sat holding the mallet, feeling its curves and angles, my father thought back to when he had visited the cemeteries in Uhrichsville in 1978. He had been especially impressed with Union Cemetery, a vast burial ground with multiple memorials to veterans from earlier wars. As he walked among those graves, he felt like he was on hallowed ground, certain that JKP was buried nearby. Pressed for time, as the sun began setting, he and my mother had to abandon their search and continue their journey back to Florida.

In the days following his re-discovery of the mallet, my father experienced disappointment that he had not found JKP's grave thirty years previously. He felt that he needed that closure before he could begin to unravel and then piece back together JKP's story.

Something strange began happening in his head. In high school, one of his football team's opponent's field was next to a cemetery. When playing that team, the home crowd's favorite defensive cheer was, "Push 'em in the cemetery; push 'em in the cemetery." Through the end of December 2003 and into early 2004, that cheer often invaded my father's thoughts. "In the cemetery, in the cemetery, in the cemetery." Over and over.

One morning, my father remembered his hunch about JKP's burial in Union Cemetery. He sat down at his computer and carefully pecked out a letter to the cemetery caretaker. He put it in the mail and was surprised to hear back within a week from Superintendent David Aldergate, informing my father that, indeed, JKP Ferrell was buried in Section B, Lot 66 of Union Cemetery.

My father experienced a surge of excitement. He felt like he was scratching the surface of a major story. The mallet had become a conduit, between him and a long forgotten Civil War soldier. His thrift shop treasure seemed to have special powers. It gave him purpose, a new mission. For the first time in years, he developed a spring in his step.

CHAPTER 4
My Father and JKP Ferrell

When my father first cleaned up the mallet thirty years previously, he thought the initials were JRP. He made some calls to Andersonville, but he came up short. At that time, there was no internet, no Google. I suspect the records at Andersonville were not well organized either.

Ed Fleming, my father's best friend from high school, drove from New Hampshire to South Florida to visit my father in early 2004, shortly after my father's rediscovery of the mallet and Mr. Aldergate's acknowledgement of Ferrell's final resting place in Union Cemetery. After showing Ed the letter he'd received from Mr. Aldergate, the two of them carefully re-examined the chiseled writing on the mallet. They realized the initial R was, indeed, a K.

A few days later, Ed contacted the Andersonville National Historic Site. The operator transferred his call to one of the curators at the museum. After a few minutes of waiting, the curator came on the line. Yes, there had been a Union Army private, John KP Ferrell, a member of the 51st Ohio Volunteer Infantry, imprisoned at Andersonville for seven months, from February 1864 through September 1864. Ed smiled at my father as he heard this news over the phone. My father—through Ed—had solved a piece of the puzzle.

With great anticipation, my father and Ed started searching the relatively nascent internet for any information about this Civil War soldier and the town in which he had been buried. Their early searches connected them with Tom Hamilton, a genealogy expert who lived in Uhrichsville and collaborated with the local Tuscarawas County Historical Society. Tom and my father became pen pals, and with help from others, they pieced together JKP's life. On a hunch, Ed Fleming surmised that the initials KP might stand for Knox Polk, the sitting U. S. president in the year that JKP was born. Ed turned out to be right. The mallet had been made by John Knox Polk Ferrell.

Through the spring of 2004, my father catalogued all the information he obtained about JKP. After multiple iterations, he penned the following manuscript, published in the summer edition of *The Chronicler*, a quarterly publication by The Tuscarawas County Historical Society. The title assigned by the newsletter was *"A Civil War Odyssey."* (I have included my father's titles as subtitles).

THE TREASURE OF UHRICHSVILLE OHIO
or
TWO BITS WON'T BUY YOU VERY MUCH:

I would like to share with you the story of a soldier of the Grand Army of the Republic, my odyssey with Pvt. JKP Ferrell of Uhrichsville, Ohio.

Road Worthy

Who I am is a minor part of the story, but it adds some flavor for if the same circumstance would have presented itself to one other than a Buckeye, perhaps this story might never have become known.

I was born in Cleveland, Ohio. In 1972, my family moved to South Florida. My eyes have always viewed with interest the rubbish piles of my neighbors on collection day. However, it was not off a rubbish pile that I found a treasure. Mind you, this was long before the Antique's Road Show. As I recall, I was at the Salvation Army Thrift Store in Pompano Beach sometime in the early to mid 70s.

There in the bric-a-brac section was a crudely carved mallet or gavel. Penned on the head was JKP Ferrell, Uhrichsville, Ohio and on the other side Andersonville, GA. I became excited. My wife and I had been to the infamous Civil War prison where more than 12,000 Union soldiers died from disease, malnutrition, overcrowding, and exposure. I had owned a lot on Johnson's Island in Sandusky Bay, Ohio and visited the Confederate prisoner of war cemetery there.

I paid my 25 cents and took the gavel home. Later I called Andersonville and described my treasure. I also wrote Washington. In short, I drew blanks. In 1978, My daughter graduated from the College of Wooster in Wooster, Ohio, and on a hunch, we drove over to Uhrichsville and walked through Union Cemetery. It was a weekend, and there was nobody to talk to and we came away empty, although I now know that JKP Ferrell and his wife are indeed buried there (Info provided by Supt. David Aldergate).

For over 30 years, the gavel was stowed away. A couple of months ago my high school buddy, Ed Fleming from Merrimac, N. Hampshire, was visiting us in S. Florida. I showed Ed the gavel that might have been made by a Union soldier at Andersonville. A week later Ed broke the log jam and informed me that JKP Ferrell had been a prisoner at Andersonville. Tom Hamilton, Tuscarawas County Genealogical Society, was particularly helpful with research and asked me to write about the odyssey.

James W. Ziegler, M.D.

The story is presented by a layperson, with a cursory look at a tiny portion of the records. I do not purport to be a historian and have reflected as best I could ascertain, a portion of the life of JKP Ferrell.

John Knox Polk Ferrell was born August 16, 1844. My friend, Ed, pointed out that James Knox Polk was elected president of the United States in 1844. JKP obviously was named after President Polk.

Shortly after turning 17, Pvt. Ferrell joined the Union Army on Sept 7, 1861. He was a private in Company A of the 51st. Ohio Vol. Infantry. He was captured at the battle of Stone River (aka Murfreesboro or Stones River) on or about Jan. 2, 1863. He was shipped to Libby Prison in Richmond, VA., later exchanged for a Rebel soldier and sent to Annapolis, where it is said he walked back to Ohio to rejoin the 51st. He later participated in the bloody battle at Chickamauga, Ga., Sept. 18-20, 1863, where he again was taken prisoner, with other members of his company, shipped to Libby Prison, transferred to Danville Prison, and then to Andersonville.

It appears he was a prisoner for over a year (with seven months at Andersonville). He escaped at Macon, Ga. He rejoined the 51st and was mustered out of service Oct. 17, 1864, as his enlistment time had expired.

On March 28, 1865, JKP reenlisted as a substitute in Co. K, 18th Ohio Regiment. Apparently, as we used to say, he found a home in the Army. It is not clear when he was finally discharged. The history of the 51st O.V.I. in the Civil War is a story of many battles and many casualties.

JKP was one of 18 children, nine girls, and nine boys. His parents were Thomas and Margaret Ferrell. Thomas, his father, joined the Union Army, Co. E, 16th Infantry Regiment, 51st O.V.I. on April 19, 1861. He drowned in the Ohio River when he fell overboard on his way to Camp Dennison. He was the first casualty of the Company.

60

It appears that two of JKP's eight brothers also joined the Army. Charles was in Company K, 69th OVI and participated in Sherman's March to the Sea. He was said to be a good soldier and was honorably discharged. I have no information on the other brother.

JKP suffered from his incarceration in Rebel prisons. He was mustered out of service and later pensioned for apparent service-related health reasons. JKP Ferrell returned to Uhrichsville and worked as a blacksmith for the Railroad Shop in Dennison. He married Lydia Wood and had one daughter, Octave. He served one year as Junior Vice Commander of the national G.A.R.

Probably most of the citizens in the Uhrichsville area know very little about JKP Ferrell. We promise never to forget those who fought for our country, but time moves on and the grave markers are weathered, and the names blurred.

When JKP died in 1929, he was the last of the 18 Ferrell children. Where was the gavel made and for what purpose? I guess it was made for me so that I could share this story with you.

They say that two bits won't buy very much.

Nicholas J Ziegler

When I read this article in the early summer of 2004, I was impressed with my father, for the research he had done and the story he had crafted. I thought the Ferrell saga was captivating, a mystery solved. I didn't think there was much more to add.

CHAPTER 5
A Modern Civil War Odyssey:
Desh Raight, Uhuh!

During late spring of 2004, I had frequent e-mail and phone conversations with my dad about the mallet and JKP. My father remained energized even after the acceptance of his narrative for publication. He started calling me in the morning on my cell phone as I commuted to work to discuss new findings, often wondering aloud about some of the missing pieces of information. He had clearly connected with JKP and yearned to know more. I became his sounding board. Because I was preoccupied with so many other things, I initially was not as enthusiastic. When he'd call, I would patiently hear him out and offer my opinions. As time passed, I was pulled in by my father's curiosity and the mystery of the mallet. I realized that to quench my father's thirst for knowledge he needed to walk in JKP's shoes. He needed to take a road trip.

My father had always been a fan of planning trips, hitting the open road, and visiting new places. When I was young, he'd throw our family into an old *Rambler* station wagon, sometimes pulling a trailer, and we'd drive for two or three weeks. During those years, we travelled out West and visited most of the national parks and major U. S. landmarks. During my teenage years, he planned trips to Europe. He did all the driving, and we usually camped or stayed in cheap guesthouses or hostels. In 1985, during my first year of pediatric residency, my father bought a van, contacted me and all my siblings, and proposed a camping trip to Alaska. In the end, my parents, my sister Edie and her husband Gary, my brother Joe, my brother-in-law Arlan, and I ended up going.

Gary and Joe drove the van to Seattle, and the rest of us flew in and met them there. We piled into the van and headed north into Canada and up Vancouver Island. We then took a long ferry boat ride through the inner passageway landing in Homer. We traveled for miles through the vast Alaskan wilderness and made it as far north as Fairbanks. It was a fun vacation, full of laughter, tasty food, late night campfires, and family bonding. Based on the Alaska trip, I suspected that other family members might be interested in another road trip.

By the summer of 2004, my father was having increasing difficulty with mobility. He slowly shuffled with the aid of a walker. When he was in a hurry or needed to cover larger stretches of ground, he allowed friends and family members to push him in a wheelchair. His tremor and muscle weakness had progressed. He often referred to himself as "the old guy with the shakes." On top of that, he needed constant access to a bathroom.

To take him on the trip I envisioned, I'd need to rent an RV; if more than a few family members decided to come along it would have to be a big one. My father would need plenty of space. After I checked out various RV models and estimated costs, I called my brother Joe and brother-in-law Arlan to see if they thought my plan was realistic and if they were interested. With no hesitation, both agreed. Joe's only request was, "Please don't let dad be in charge of supplies."

I laughed, again thinking back to our Alaska trip. My dad had assured Joe and me that we needn't worry about supplies. He would procure sleeping bags, lanterns, stove, ponchos, coolers, etc. We were both busy, I with residency and Joe still in college, so we appreciated his offer. What we didn't consider was my father's approach to provisioning. He most definitely did not subscribe to the adage that "you get what you pay for." His philosophy was "the cheaper the better, and then you make do." All the equipment he had purchased at cut rate prices did not hold up, and we ended up throwing most of it away within the first days of the trip and purchasing new gear that actually worked.

Because I spoke with Joe and Arlan first, the RV adventure turned into a guys' trip. We invited my other brother-in-law Gary, but he was too busy finishing jobs with his landscaping business in Colorado. So, it looked like the travelers would be my dad, Arlan, Joe, and me, though David, Arlan's 26-year-old son and my oldest nephew, intimated that he might want to come along. He was afraid to commit, I think uncomfortable with the prospect of confinement for a week in a motorhome with four crazy older relatives, including his father and grandfather.

I called my dad and proposed a motorhome trip starting in South Florida. I'd fly down, and we'd make Andersonville, Chickamauga, Stones River, and Uhrichsville our priorities. We would find JKP's grave. To give everyone a few months to plan, I suggested October. The weather would still be warm but not too hot, and the summer vacation crowds would be back in school. The roads and sites we hoped to visit would be less congested. I could tell my dad was excited at the prospect of taking part in an adventure that he had initiated by finding and then researching the mallet.

With only a week to cover an ambitious distance, we knew we needed to be organized. I told my dad to plan the itinerary. I'd arrange for a motorhome; Joe and Arlan would work on supplies. Over the next few months, the four of us talked often. My dad developed a preliminary schedule.

My brother Joe turned forty just before our departure. He lived in Boca Raton, Florida, down the street from my parents. At that time, he was building an environmental engineering business. He'd been very successful during the early years of this venture, and he plowed every extra cent he earned back into his business. He accumulated no debt as he grew from two to seven employees. During his master's work at the University of Florida, he had devised a system for cleaning up Florida's polluted sandy soil and the shallow water table just below the ground's surface. He commercialized this system and started decontaminating small hazardous waste sites including former gas stations, dry cleaners, and other "mom and pop" operations. As he expanded his business, the projects became more complex and included airports and major industrial sites. He worked long hours most days of the week, and though he loved his job, it clearly interfered with his main passions in life, building and rigging boats and fishing. At the time of the trip, Joe was married and had a five-year-old son, Nicholas, named after my father.

Joe is many things rolled into one—funny, tough, fearless at times, multi-talented, big hearted. He can do anything, and he doesn't take shit from anyone. He's an aggressive, unforgiving driver, and he borders on being just a little crazy, especially when it comes to fishing.

I remember fishing Sebastian Inlet just south of Melbourne, Florida with him one September weekend in the late eighties during the fall finger mullet run. Fishermen were lined up along the jetty, casting out into schools of redfish, snook, and tarpon feeding in the outgoing tide. The action was nonstop. A couple of fishermen wandered too close to us, and Joe told them they needed to move. They didn't listen and began casting over our lines, an unforgivable sin in Joe's book. One of the guys looked like a professional NFL lineman.

His friend was not much smaller. Next thing I knew, Joe screamed at the bigger guy to stop casting over our lines. The situation deteriorated, and a few seconds later I looked over and found Joe and this guy trading profanities and having a sword fight with with their fishing poles. I couldn't help but laugh to myself at the ridiculous sight of two grown men trying to hit each other with their flimsy fishing poles. But I was also terrified that we were going to get our asses kicked. After a brief battle, the guy sensed that Joe was just a little too crazy to mess with and retreated. The yelling and flailing stopped, and the two trespassers grabbed their gear and moved out of our sight. Joe re-baited his line and resumed fishing, unfazed by the altercation—just another day on the jetty. Do not get between Joe and fish.

Arlan was 59 years old at the time of the trip. He was originally from Indiana. After attending a small Lutheran college in rural Nebraska (where I think he spent most of his time hunting), he graduated with an education degree and started out as a teacher, first in upstate New York, where it took him less than two years to realize he hated northeastern winters. When he saw an advertisement for a job at a newly opened Lutheran school in Deerfield Beach, Florida, he jumped at the opportunity. He landed the job as principal and taught science at the same time my sister Ellen graduated from college and also secured a teaching job there. He eventually worked up the courage to ask her out, and their relationship grew. Arlan and Ellen got married my first year of college, and they later had three boys.

Arlan loved the outdoors and was almost as passionate about fishing as my brother. With time, he and Joe became hard core fishing buddies, often leaving the dock at 5 am and returning after dark, usually with a boat filled with fish.

In some ways, Arlan was bigger than life to me, kind of a second father figure. He was always happy, telling jokes, looking for humor in the direst situation. He had a mischievous, snickering laugh that was infectious, and once he got me going, I could laugh for hours, sometimes with him, but mostly at him and that contagious laugh. During the Alaska trip, he, Joe, and I shared a tent, and I can remember laughing ourselves to sleep each night as he told joke after joke, interrupted by hilarious one-liners from Joe.

In his forties, Arlan decided to switch careers. He continued to teach but also started attending law school. After obtaining his law degree, he took over and then built up my parents' old law practice.

A few years before our motorhome trip, doctors had diagnosed him with polycythemia vera, a bone marrow disease characterized by excessive red blood cell production (the opposite of anemia). Too many red blood cells thicken the blood, and Arlan had to undergo phlebotomy monthly to keep his blood count regulated as close to normal as possible. He didn't let this problem affect his daily life or his positive attitude. He went with the flow, accepting what life threw at him. Anyone who didn't know him well would never guess he had a serious, chronic blood disorder.

I was almost forty-seven when I began planning our odyssey. I was well into my career as a pediatric cardiologist, the director of a growing division. My daughters were six and eleven years old, and I hated the thought of leaving my wife and kids for a week. This trip would challenge me. Starting off, I had three goals—to take my 76-year-old father on what would probably be his last road trip, to get him through it and back to my mother, and then to safely return to my family in Rhode Island.

During the months leading up to the motorhome trip, I was busy at work and time passed quickly. Summer eased into fall, my kids went back to school, the temperature started dropping, and the leaves began to change. The Red Sox were playing the Yankees for the American League championship, and when I departed Rhode Island late Friday, October 15th, 2004, the Sox were behind two games to none. I had lofty expectations for this team, convinced that 2004 would finally be Boston's year.

Johnny Damon, Boston's center fielder, was in the midst of a wicked hitting slump, and I remember talking to my dad the night before I flew down to Florida. My dad didn't like Damon, mostly because of his 1960's style "mullet" hair-do. When he ran, Damon's hair flew in all directions. For some reason, despite my father's love of individuality and dislike of conformity and "answering to the man," long hair on men never sat well with him. That night on the phone, as we completed plans and arranged for my pick-up at the Fort Lauderdale airport, we discussed the ALCS. I tried to convince my father that Johnny Damon was a great baseball player. It was to no avail. My dad's reply was, "He's a bum." I told him not to lose faith, that the Red Sox were still in this series. He thought they'd get swept in four games.

The trip officially commenced when I walked out of the Fort Lauderdale Airport at around 11 pm and found Arlan, Joe, and my dad, elbows sticking out their respective windows, waiting in Joe's truck. I threw my gear into the bed and hopped into the back seat and sat next to Arlan. My dad rode shotgun. The three glanced at me and gave a nod. Few words were exchanged as we drove away. We were all tired but shared a discernible feeling of excitement and mystery. We were teammates about to embark on a week-long odyssey, not at all sure what it would bring. My dad dubbed us "the fantastic four."

It was midnight when Joe dropped my father and me at my parents' house. I could tell my dad was excited. He showed me the finalized version of his article, and we talked about our tentative plan for the next day: pick up the motorhome early, run by Walmart and a grocery store for supplies and food, and depart South Florida by early afternoon. My mom emerged from her bedroom and fixed me a bowl of cut up fruit. She then showed me my bed. I was exhausted and fell asleep within seconds. Though I missed my three girls, it felt comfortable being home with my parents.

Joe and Arlan greeted me when I opened my eyes the next morning. After inhaling extra-large coffees, we headed down to Fort

Lauderdale to pick up our 32-foot, class A motorhome. I hadn't had much time to research all the specs on the model we were renting, but I knew it had a private suite in the back with a queen-sized bed, which I thought would be perfect for accommodating my father. The rear suite was only a few steps from the bathroom. The rest of us would make do in the front, either on seats which converted to pop-out beds, one single and one double, or on air-mattresses on the floor.

At the RV center, I signed all the paperwork. The rental agent led us out to our *"Chalet"* model. The interior was spacious, clean and comfortable. Although not luxurious, it was more than adequate for the four of us. It had a medium sized refrigerator, a two-burner gas stove, an oven, and a microwave. Everything seemed to work. There was also plenty of storage for cookware, towels, bedding, and other daily necessities. Behind the two front seats were a couch on one side and a swivel chair on the other.

After our motorhome training and orientation, Arlan left in his car for home. I hoisted myself up into the driver's seat, and Joe climbed into the passenger seat. Visibility out the front window was limitless. Sitting up high, we felt like truckers about to hit the open road. I put the vehicle into drive and headed for the exit.

There was a slight descent from the parking area to the four-lane highway we needed to enter. Traffic was heavy, and we had to wait for clearance, the nose of our vehicle pointing downward. Joe grew increasingly impatient and started urging me to hit it every time there was a slight break. Having no idea of the acceleration or turning radius of the RV, I was uncomfortable blasting out into the oncoming traffic.

After waiting for several minutes, an opening appeared. I pressed the accelerator, and the RV lurched forward. The back end, which hung out well past the rear wheels, made a loud screeching noise as the undercarriage smacked down on the exit ramp and dragged across the cement. It felt like we were either going to get stuck with half the motorhome hanging out into traffic or it was going to split in two. Thankfully, neither happened, and after a few seconds that felt like endless minutes, the noise stopped, the RV heaved forward, and we turned onto the highway toward home.

Driving was initially awkward, but I rapidly adjusted to the oversized vehicle that would be our home for the next week. When we arrived at my parents' house, I parked the RV in their driveway. Joe and I got out and walked to the rear of the vehicle. Two struts pointed down behind the back tires, both compressed and bent inward. I pictured my $500 deposit trashed, a "goner."

Joe looked over at me and said, "Good thing you're a doctor."

He then started shaking his head in the affirmative, as if he had come to some great revelation, and, with a voice combining Gomer Pyle and Jed Clampett into one, exclaimed, "Desh raight."

I couldn't help but laugh at what was clearly his latest profound saying, something so simple, applicable to any circumstance, but only if uttered with the right accents and intonations. For the next week, whenever the situation fit, Joe would emphasize any point he was making with "desh raight." Every time he did, Arlan, my dad, and I laughed…for about five minutes!

Shortly after our arrival, Arlan came down to my parents' house with my nephew David. Upon seeing the motorhome and sensing the upcoming adventure, David decided he was in. With this spontaneous decision, the "fantastic four" became the "fabulous five." Joe and I told David he was welcome to come, but that he'd have to share the double bed with Arlan AND he'd have to take responsibility for hooking up water and septic at the campsites each night and disconnecting in the morning. David wasn't thrilled about the latter job.

"Why do I get the shit job?" he asked.

Joe responded, "Because you're the youngest, and you need to respect your elders. Now you can either come and handle all the shit or you can stay here with your mommy while the real men take this machine on a memorable journey."

"Desh raight," I piped in.

David reluctantly agreed to our terms.

We decided to divide and conquer. Joe, Arlan, David, and I would hit Costco and Walmart for food and supplies. My mom, sister Ellen, and dad would outfit the RV with cookware, utensils, pillows, bedding, towels, tools, and other household items.

The four of us left my parents around 10:30 am. I anticipated we would return in no more than two hours and hopefully load up and begin our journey north by early afternoon. We had made a list of basic food items that included Snickers, salami, pancake mix, bacon, eggs, baked beans, and hot dogs. There was complete consensus on those items. The rest was up for grabs.

We hit Walmart first. We needed an air mattress, flashlights, toiletries, camping items, a few small propane tanks for Joe's grill, and various other odds and ends. I wanted to get in and out quickly, and I'd hoped we could split the list of items and then reconvene. I had not anticipated the science applied to shopping by the duo of Arlan and David. They dissected and compared every item before deciding which to purchase. Joe and I felt like we were with two grandmothers. Buying flashlights turned into a half hour affair. And then getting batteries took even longer. Each item required intense discussion. I became increasingly impatient, and as Arlan and David argued over the best toilet paper for the motorhome, I could hold back no longer.

"You two grannies do know that we have to drive that friggin' tank of a motorhome to Ohio and back in seven days, right? Can you please just grab some toilet paper. We need to hit the road."

Arlan looked at David, then me, and asked, "Well, this toilet paper is two ply and still cheaper than all the rest. What do you think?"

Before David could answer, I replied, "I will wipe my ass with sandpaper if it gets me out of here sooner."

71

I heard Arlan's snickering laugh as I grabbed my items and followed the other three to the cashier.

After checking out, we headed to Costco for groceries. Navigation down the packed aisles was difficult, especially since each of us was pushing a cart. We filled all four with food, grabbing things randomly, four dudes, impulse buying at its finest, and in bulk no less. We made sure we had all the goodies my father enjoyed since he wasn't there to represent himself.

Between the precision shopping at Walmart and the bounty of food bought at Costco fighting the frenzied South Florida mob of Saturday afternoon shoppers, we didn't get back to Boca until 3:30 pm. The team at my parents' house had provisioned the RV with most of the necessities on our list. We packed our added items and the food into remaining storage areas. By 5 pm, everything was stowed. We decided we'd leave that evening.

After quick goodbyes, I jumped into the driver's seat, David into the passenger seat, and the other three found places in the back. I carefully backed out of the driveway as my mom, Ellen, Joe's wife Lisa, and Joe's son Nick waved to us. Nick held back tears. He so wanted to be one of the guys going on the motorhome trip. He thought the RV was the coolest thing he'd ever seen.

We headed west out of Boca and then north on Interstate-95. When we reached cruising speed, I felt free, totally in control, certain that I could steer our machine wherever this trip might take us. My confidence was replaced by terror as the first 18-wheeler sped past. The motorhome shook violently and then jerked to the right, the steering wheel almost ripped out of my hands. "Holy shit," I yelled. I gripped the steering wheel tightly as a line of semi's flew by. Each one caused the RV to shudder, vibrate, and then pull to the right. Eventually, I perfected the nuances of driving. I became adept at anticipating and smoothing out the effects of passing traffic. Confidence slowly crept back. Blood flow returned to my knuckles.

North of West Palm Beach, we picked up the Florida Turnpike. We continued north to Wildwood and then merged onto I-75. We drove for five straight hours, engaged in animated conversation, passing around snack foods and drinks. The energy level was high, and time flew by. Near Gainesville, we briefly pulled off the highway to change drivers, and Joe assumed the driver's seat.

I sat in back with my dad and Arlan. I knew the Red Sox were playing the Yankees that night in game three of the ALCS, and I asked David to turn on the radio and see if he could find the game. He tried but no luck. Joe seemed comfortable behind the wheel, and I was happy to relax. Joe asked David to put a video tape he had brought with him into the VCR that was attached to a small television set hanging from the ceiling in front of the passenger seat.

Joe had filmed a recent hurricane that had wreaked havoc on south Florida. As we sped north at 70 mph, passing cars and sharing the road with 18-wheelers, Joe began pointing at the television screen, gesticulating wildly, and narrating the hurricane scenes. His eyes darted from the road to the screen and then back again. I was terrified. My third goal of this trip—surviving and making it home to my family—seemed to be in jeopardy as the motorhome ran up on cars, passed them, and swerved in and out of the breakdown and passing lanes. No one else seemed bothered. I suggested that we view the video another time, but the others were intrigued by Joe's adventure—footage caught in the heart of a Category 4 hurricane. They watched intently. They'd all lived through it. Not wanting to insult Joe, I gave in. I remember thinking two things. First, I really didn't have any control over my destiny. I would survive this trip if it was in the cards. Second, the next time I got control of the driver's seat, I would not relinquish it.

We crossed into Georgia just after midnight. I asked David to look in the road atlas (*remember, this trip preceded smart phones*) to see if there were any RV parks coming up. He searched the local map and found the Valdosta/Lake Park KOA, ten miles ahead.

David navigated to our first night's encampment which was adjacent to the interstate, separated from the shoulder only by a chain link fence and narrow access road.

There were signs directing late arrivals, and we found a spot and pulled in. We noticed other signs emphasizing "quiet times." Though we did our best to respect our slumbering neighbors, we couldn't keep from banging into each other in the dark, dropping objects, and knocking things over. There was a fifteen-minute continuous barrage of "shit", "damn it", followed by someone shushing, inevitably followed by Arlan's snickering laugh that then had us all laughing, then shushing, and then laughing more.

Because we were so disorganized and trying our best to be quiet, it took twice as long to get situated. We first settled my dad in his rear suite. The rest of us arranged the front area for sleeping. I inflated my air mattress and stretched it between a pop-out make-shift bed on the port side where Arlan and David slept, and a smaller bed on the starboard side occupied by Joe. My air mattress was not high quality. It was flimsy and noisy.

By 1:30 am, we began drifting off to sleep. It was not peaceful. There was ongoing traffic noise as trucks barreled by on the interstate no more than 100 yards away. Arlan fell asleep and began snoring…loudly! And every time I moved on the air mattress, it sounded like fireworks exploding. Thankfully, my dad's suite had a door which partially blocked him from the din in the forward cabin. Eventually we drifted off, but sleep was sporadic. At 4:30 am, a rooster began crowing; shortly after, our neighbors on both sides awakened and exacted revenge for our previous night's disrespect for "quiet time."

I didn't realize it at the time, but my father kept a small diary of the trip. The following reflects some of his thoughts about our first day:

When does the journey begin? We talk about doing things in life, but most of the time our thoughts do not materialize into action.

Road Worthy

The dye was cast when Jim reserved a 32-foot RV for October 16-23, 2004. Between my shakes, I made up a rough itinerary.

It looked like all systems were go when Jim arrived from Rhode Island. Most of the participants and I had camped together for 3 weeks during a wonderful trip to Alaska in 1985. I had been invited to make the present trip because of my discovery of a mallet made by JKP Ferrell, a Civil War soldier. JKP had been captured twice, at the battle of Stones River in Tennessee and later at the bloody battle of Chickamauga Georgia. The second time he was imprisoned at Andersonville, so we had three important sites to visit.

As we prepare to leave, we are hopeful that our digital cameras, camcorder, laptop, and cell phones come through and work properly when called upon. As I write this, the boys are out shopping for supplies and food. Already we are finding things to laugh about. For instance, Joe says our RV gets one mile per gallon. He says we will be filling our 75-gallon tank every hour, so we will get to see lots of gas stations.

Our main staples on our Alaska trip were Snickers bars and salami sandwiches. We OD'd on these nutritional items, but we are all game to OD on these same victuals again. It makes meal planning easy.

The motorhome is quite elegant, way beyond any of my past camping trips. It appears that my grandson David is coming along. We are now a merry band of five. David had been invited earlier, but there was no clear decision until the last minute when we became the "Fabulous Five." Well, maybe me and a Fabulous Four, my contribution being minimal.

The first day's travel went smoothly with David doing most of the navigating. I felt very lucky to be on this trip. To have no responsibility is Hog Heaven. At times, I felt like a passenger on a train. My only regret is that other family members do not get to be a part of this adventure. We hope we can share effectively our experience, and if we accomplish that, we add another bonus.

Around midnight we found a KOA at Valdosta Lake Park in Lake Park, GA. We were pretty smug about our RV until we saw some of the monsters in the KOA park.

By isolating me, the rest of the group got some sleep under crowded and less than luxurious conditions. I did not sleep much. Jim's air mattress, a level one bargain, sounded like "thunder and awe" every time he shifted position.

CHAPTER 6
On to Andersonville

Around 6 am, we got up and stumbled outside. Joe extracted his gas grill from the outdoor storage compartment and David hooked up the water line. It was chilly, clear but with fog traipsing over the ground. We carried a picnic table and set it outside the door of our rig. Arlan poured coffee, just as my dad made an appearance. We helped him down the stairs leading outside to a seat at the table.

My dad was in good spirits, though he hadn't slept any better than the rest of us. I gave him his medications and his morning banana (my mom's order). We then wolfed down a breakfast fit for kings, everything ready in a perfectly coordinated fashion. Not bad for five sleep-deprived guys.

After breakfast, we sat and discussed tactics. Should we head to Andersonville and then visit other key spots on the way to Ohio or race to Ohio and then stop at important sites on the way back?

We were close to Andersonville, just a little over two hours away. I think because we sensed this proximity and were very excited to see Andersonville, we decided to make it our first stop. By 10 am, we were on the road. Next stop: the site of JKP's longest Civil War incarceration as a POW.

Before we reached the entrance to I-75 north, I saw a small convenience store. I pulled into the parking lot and informed my mates that I wanted to get a newspaper to see how the Red Sox had made out the night before. I ran in and found a local paper with a summary and box score of game 3 of the ALCS. I climbed back into the motorhome and handed the paper to my dad.

"Dad, read me the game summary and box," I asked.

My dad opened the paper. "Well, the Red Sox got their asses kicked 18 to 9. They are now down three to zip. Who gives up eighteen runs in a championship series?"

I felt so sure that the Red Sox would break the "Curse of the Bambino" this year that I turned around, looked at my father, and proclaimed, "The Sox are gonna take this series."

My dad laughed. "I don't think any team has come back from three losses to win." He then ran through the box score.

I asked, "How did my man Damon do?"

My dad replied, "The bum finally got a hit. Maybe if he got a haircut, he could see the ball."

It was Damon's first hit of the series. I knew the Sox needed his bat to have any chance at coming back. I worried that my dad was right; it would take a miracle. What I didn't know was that David Ortiz, their designated hitter, was about to go on an unprecedented post-season hitting streak.

There were two routes into Andersonville from our starting point. One involved travel on backroads. We decided that was our best (and probably most scenic) option. With David navigating, I turned off the interstate onto a two-lane country road that weaved through cotton farms, pecan groves, and tiny rural hamlets. In most of the fields, workers stood, bent over picking cotton. From the road, we saw the white clusters shining in the morning sun. It was a vibrant day, clear blue sky with little humidity.

As I drove through the South Georgia countryside, my nephew David in the passenger seat, the five of us engaged in lively conversation, I felt completely at peace. It was one of those unique moments in life, the experience vividly memorable to me even today.

As we neared Andersonville, we came upon a roadside stand selling produce. We pulled off, got out of the RV, stretched our legs, and bought some peaches and apples. David wanted to try driving, so I let him take the wheel to bring us into Andersonville. I was impressed with the care he applied to maneuvering the motorhome; the ride was so smooth that I relaxed and lost myself in the passing vistas.

David carefully negotiated a left turn onto the access road to Andersonville. We were speechless as we looked out on the expansive open farmland, so very green this time of the year. The place was deceptively alluring—so much history and so much suffering.

Just before reaching the Visitor Center, the road split and the incoming lane banked to the right. As I remember it, the road was newly paved, flat blacktop, but David's speed coming into the split was a little fast, and he took the right turn slightly too hard. The motorhome shuddered and temporarily felt like it was on two wheels. Everyone leaned to the left. David tried to correct and jerked the steering wheel back to the left. As David remembers it, the road was gravel, bumpy, and imperfectly banked. Though he tried to carefully negotiate the slight right turn, the uneven road caused the motorhome to lean to the right and then shimmy back to the left.

Either way, as the motorhome overcorrected back to the left, items flew out of cupboards, drawers, and lockers. Plates crashed onto counters and then the floor. Cooking utensils rocketed through the air and hit the opposite wall. The refrigerator door swung open, and we watched a six-pack of beer bang against the swinging door and then hurdle across the sink, followed by sandwich items and condiments. Food, cans, bottles, paper towels, batteries, flashlights, and paperware scattered everywhere. Thankfully, nobody was injured and nothing broke.

David pulled the motorhome to a stop. He seemed frozen in the driver's seat, gripping the wheel and staring straight ahead as if temporarily dazed. The rest of us sat in stunned silence, surveying the mess and wondering what the hell had just happened. Did we almost flip the RV? We looked at each other for a few seconds, no one speaking, and then we began laughing. David turned around and joined in. Every time the laughter ebbed, Arlan snickered, and the rest of us involuntarily started up again. The laughter continued until most of us, including my dad, had tears streaming down our faces.

I finally collected myself and suggested, "Maybe I should drive."

Joe agreed. "Desh Raight." Those two words had us laughing for another five minutes as David tried to defend his driving. He finally gave up and joined the chorus.

I slowly pulled into the parking lot. Joe and Arlan picked up the loose items and restored order as my dad, wiping tears and trying to hold back laughter, looked on. I parked away from the main entrance. We made some sandwiches and then sat in our mobile abode with windows and door open. As we ate our lunch, a cooling breeze circulated through the enclosed space.

The Andersonville Welcome Center and Museum were clean and well kept. Behind the more modern buildings was a small rebuilt remnant of the old stockade walls with the mostly missing sections mapped out by white posts. There was a second line of white posts twenty feet in from the outer stockade posts depicting the "deadline": the inner off-limit area next to the stockade walls. Guards perched high atop the walls had orders to shoot on sight prisoners who wandered across that line.

A paved road encircled the area of imprisonment with frequent pull-offs to allow visitors to park, get out, and walk the grounds of the POW camp. Behind the visitors' station, we looked out at the original twenty acres of confinement. An open grassy field sloped down to a swampy section separated by a slow running brook.

Andersonville—the most notorious POW camp of the Civil War—a twenty-acre rectangular stockade surrounding south Georgian open ground, originally built to house 10,000 men to help with the overflow of prisoners in Richmond. When the walls went up, the Union and Confederacy were still exchanging prisoners; Andersonville was to be a temporary holding pen. There was no time or manpower to build shelters, so captured soldiers would be exposed to cold, rain, oppressive heat, and the unforgiving summer sun, sleeping under whatever shelters could be fashioned from the items they brought in with them. The small creek running through the stockade was the only source of water, but the designers situated the cook house and Confederate barracks above the inflow section, polluting the stream before it flowed into the camp.

The Confederacy did not anticipate that the Union would end prisoner exchanges; that Lincoln and Grant would conclude that this war could only be won by attrition. No one knew that the intensity of battle would escalate, that the number of confined prisoners in Andersonville would exceed 40,000 at its zenith, that disease would run rampant, that one in three prisoners would die. No one foresaw that the broken Confederacy, barely able to equip its own troops, would never be able to care for and feed such a vast number of captive soldiers, many already injured and badly broken before passing through the entrance gates.

Leaders in Washington knew the state of affairs in Andersonville, but they were more intent on winning the war. They ignored it. They considered the 100-plus men dying each day to be casualties of war, no more and no less important than soldiers dying on the battlefield.

Andersonville—a place where the worst and best came out in men. Thugs, banding together and preying on the weak, stealing food and supplies. Others rendering aid to sick and dying comrades, putting their own lives in jeopardy—starving, but giving away food; wet and cold but covering a weaker friend. Despite the horrific conditions, for most of the suffering prisoners, allegiance, love, compassion, and honor still prevailed.

As I gazed out at the peaceful landscape, these thoughts flooded my mind.

My brother stood next to me staring ahead, speechless. He looked over at me and asked. "How the hell did that slight, simple, teenage farm boy from Ohio survive this place?"

I had to admit, "No clue, man."

We spent the next two hours wandering the grounds, the five of us moving in slow motion with my dad. We observed people dressed in Civil War uniforms with a film crew, a partial re-enactment. We then made our way over to the cemetery to explore the burial ground for 13,000 Union soldiers. Thankfully, a small group of prisoners had made it a priority to keep records and catalogue the dead. After the war, individual marble grave markers were erected.

Off the main burial ground, next to a big shade tree were six graves, clearly set apart—the notorious leaders of the Raiders, a group of prisoners who beat and murdered their fellow Union soldiers and stole from them. A group of brave and able men eventually banded together and said ENOUGH. They captured the Raiders, tried them, and sentenced the six most treacherous ones to hang. The trial, sentencing, and hanging all took place *within the prison walls.* I wondered if JKP might have designed the mallet for the judge who presided over the trial.

We looked at the six graves which listed each perpetrator's name and state. One of the six Raiders was from Rhode Island. Joe looked over at me, shaking his head. Under his breath, he muttered, "F'ing Rhode Islanders."

My dad, usually one to eschew profanity, couldn't help but use the opportunity to comment about the damn liberal majority in the New England states. Somehow, the fact that one of the raiders was from Rhode Island translated into the modern day "blueness" of the state, at least in his mind. I didn't see the connection, but I kept quiet.

Joe looked up. "Desh Raight."

I couldn't help but smile. I then looked down at the tombstones. I wondered what I would have done if exposed, starving, cold, and homesick? Would I maintain my moral compass with suffering and deprivation defining my daily existence? Would I retain my sense of allegiance knowing that my country had abandoned me? What measures would I have resorted to in order to survive and return to my family? The Raiders had clearly crossed the line, but I suspected they were mostly victims of desperate circumstances.

We slowly made our way back to the motorhome. Arlan drove. From the parking lot, we followed the paved road that encircled the original stockade. We stopped often, and Joe and I jumped out and walked the grounds as Arlan, David, and my father watched, slowly trailing us in the RV.

Monuments were scattered throughout the enclosed field, commissioned by various states to memorialize those who had perished here. We walked along the small stream and the marshy terrain leading down to it. We tried to envision the crowded mass of men, hear the groans of their suffering, smell the stench. The more we walked over the peaceful site, the more surreal it felt. I then came to the jarring realization that we were stepping over the same ground that Ferrell had walked upon 150 years earlier. The passage of time and change in circumstances were suddenly irrelevant. It came down to geography. We were at the exact place on earth where Ferrell had been so brutally tested. We needed to be here, to sense his anguish, feel the connection, and fully understand Ferrell's story. Joe and I looked at each other, I think simultaneously coming to the same realization. We turned and walked back to the motorhome to join the others. When I entered, my dad glanced up, and with a worried look stated, "You look like you've seen a ghost."

I replied, "I think I felt JKP's presence. It was like he was guiding me over HIS ground."

We left Andersonville around 3 pm and headed northeast. We passed through a few small towns before merging onto the interstate. I was driving again, partly because I'd gone to college in Atlanta and knew how to navigate through the city, which stood between us and Chickamauga, our next destination. Also, partly because I was hesitant to let others drive after earlier experiences. David sat next to me as my official navigator.

Our conversation mostly centered around Ferrell and Andersonville. My dad relayed what he knew about Ferrell. We didn't have a picture of him, but my father had found information suggesting that he was small in stature, around 5 foot 5 inches tall and 140 pounds in weight. He, along with his fellow infantry soldiers, carried a 55-pound field pack. We pictured this barely 17-year-old kid, lugging his pack, struggling to keep up with his fellow soldiers as he trudged south from one encampment to the next. We hoped we'd find where he'd fought at the two battle sites we were planning to visit and surmise how the Rebels captured him. It was rumored that some Civil War soldiers intentionally lingered near the rear, where they were less likely to be shot at, but more likely to be captured. We refused to believe this true of our young hero, especially since he had survived Andersonville and then voluntarily signed up again when his term with the 51st OVI expired.

It is clear that with initial incarceration, Union prisoners at Andersonville expected repatriation in short order. They had no idea of the policy change endorsed by their leaders in Washington and relayed to generals on the battlefield. In time and with rumors circulating from incoming soldiers, their hope for exchange was replaced by the biting reality that their imprisonment was indefinite.

William Comfort, a Union soldier with the 35th New Jersey Volunteers, imprisoned in Andersonville in 1864, penned a moving poem entitled *"A Cry from Andersonville Prison."* It relays the essence of survival, the grim circumstances, and the growing frustration and feeling of hopelessness. My dad had a copy of it, and as we rode northward, he pulled it out and read it to us.

"When our country called for men we came from forge and hill,
From workshop, farm, and factory the broken ranks to fill,
We left our quiet happy home and those we loved so well
But now in prison drear we languish and 'tis our constant cry,
Oh ye who yet can save us, will you leave us here to die?

Did the voice of slander tell ye that our hearts were weak with fear?
That all, or nearly all, of us were captured in the rear?
But the scars upon our bodies from the musket ball and shell,
The missing legs and shattered arms, a truer tale will tell;
We have tried to do our duty in the sight of God on high,
And ye who can yet save us, now leave us here to die.

There are hearts with hope still beating in our "Northern Homes"
Watching, waiting for the footsteps that will never come.
In "Southern prisons" pining, meager, tattered, pale and gaunt,
Growing weaker, weaker daily from pinching cold and want
Are husbands, sons and brothers who hopeless captive lie,
And ye who yet can save us, will you leave us here to die?

From out our prison gate there's a graveyard close at hand,
Where lay fourteen thousand Union men beneath a Southern sand,
And scores are laid beside them as day succeeds each day,
And thus it shall be until we all shall pass away;

And the last can say while dying with upturned glazing eye,
Both faith and love are dead at home and they've left us here to die."

Despite his gruff exterior, my dad was a gentle soul, tender hearted and easily moved. He paused several times during the reading of Comfort's poem to collect himself. We remained silent, touched by my dad's show of emotions; we felt the author's anguish. It saddened us to realize that these brave men languished in this far off prison and felt forgotten and betrayed by their leaders.

We stayed on I-75 straight through downtown Atlanta. As we passed into the city's northern suburbs, the sun began to set. I told David to look in the Atlas and find a campground. We were about fifteen miles south of *Red Top Mountain State Park.* The Atlas advertised camping and RV sites, so we decided to end our day there.

We turned onto the park access road, and the surroundings were striking. Large trees, glassy lakes, and rocky hills merged into small mountains. We reached the campground entrance at 6:15 pm only to find the posted campground hours 9 am to 6 pm. There was a locked gate, no way to drive to a campsite.

As we sat in our vehicle contemplating our options, a friendly park ranger appeared from a small building, walked over to us, and welcomed us to the park. He opened the gate and guided us to a site that sat on a woody hill overlooking a crystal-clear lake. We backed into our assigned space. No one else was around. Because the ranger had no paperwork, he told us not to worry about payment; he left us with a cheery good night. We felt incredibly fortunate for having found such a scenic spot, in October, after closing hour.

Coming through Atlanta, I had listened to a sports station that highlighted game four of the ALCS, scheduled to begin sometime after 8 pm at Boston's Fenway Park. The consensus from the sports pundits mirrored my father's sentiment. The Red Sox were as good as done. No team had ever come back to win a seven-game series after losing the first three games, and the ass-kicking the Red Sox suffered the night before suggested that the Yankees carried all the momentum. In short, everyone thought the Yankees had the series in the bag. I still had faith in the Sox, and I was eager to watch game four that night.

We arranged the interior of the motorhome for sleeping, made a campfire outside, and set up Joe's two-burner gas stove nearby on a picnic table. It was chilly, in the fifties, but clear and still. We cooked outdoors—spiced-up baked beans in a big saucepan on one burner and grilled sausages on the other. Joe manned the grill while Arlan strummed the guitar around the campfire and the rest of us sang along. We were famished. We ate the sausages in buns with mustard, and Joe, Arlan, and I washed our meals down with a few cold beers.

After dinner, I turned on our little television. For a few hours, we got spotty reception and watched part of the game. In the bottom of the seventh inning, the Red Sox were down 4-3. Mariana Rivera, one of the best closers in the history of baseball, was warming up for the Yankees. Things looked bleak.

Because they thought the game (and series) was over, my fellow campers made me find a channel with better reception. Selections were few, but we discovered the movie "The Alamo" and watched it for a while. Despite the intense on-screen drama, we were so exhausted that soon everyone climbed into sleeping bags and fell asleep. I was the last man standing. I tried switching back to the game, but reception was too poor. With hope fading, I turned off the television. I feared the Red Sox had reached the end of the road. They had never previously come back against Rivera in a playoff game. I couldn't help but once again think, "Maybe next year." I settled into my sleeping bag and fell soundly asleep.

CHAPTER 7
Chickamauga

We awoke Monday morning, October 18, 2004 at around 8 am. After our first night of little sleep followed by the emotional experience at Andersonville, we slept like babies. By this time, the motorhome reeked, the smell a combination of cooked food, sweaty socks, wet towels, nasty shoes, and five guys in a confined space who had eaten a potful of beans the night before. The smell was the first thing that struck me as I opened my eyes. The second was the beauty outside. From my vantage point looking up from the floor out the side windows, I saw a deeply blue sky with towering pines reaching upward. I could tell the air outside was still and dry, the sun warm. I wondered if JKP ever awakened in an encampment similarly awed by the spectacle of nature around him.

Everyone seemed to rouse at the same time, and we stayed in our berths and discussed the previous two days. We joked and laughed, my dad joining in from his luxury suite in the rear. We were collectively in high spirits, and everyone, including my dad, looked well rested. We ate breakfast and then lingered at the picnic table next to our RV sipping coffee. Hidden among the tall pines overlooking the reflecting lake, we planned the day's travels. The sun filtered through the trees and warmed us.

After breakfast, we explored the campground, took showers, dressed, cleaned the dishes, and packed up. At around 11 am, we hit the road—a much later start than we had planned, but nobody seemed to care.

I was excited about the day ahead. I looked forward to visiting the Civil War battle sites and finding the spots where Ferrell had been captured. I also hung on to a glimmer of hope that the Red Sox had come back the evening before. I turned on the radio but couldn't find a news or sports channel that came in clearly. After an hour of driving, we pulled off the highway to fuel up, and as Joe pumped gas, I ran into the convenience store. No newspapers—shit! I asked the storekeeper if he knew the outcome of the previous night's baseball game, but he was clearly not a sports enthusiast.

Once back on the interstate, I called Joy on my cell phone. It was her day off from work, and I caught her after a three-mile walk-run. All was well at home, both girls busy with school and sports. I asked her about the previous night's baseball game. She had watched it in its entirety. The Red Sox had come back in the bottom of the ninth inning to tie the game, and in the bottom of the twelfth, David Ortiz—Big Pappi—hit a two run, walk-off homer to keep the Red Sox's hopes alive. My intuition had been right. My fellow adventurers didn't share my enthusiasm, but they were Marlins fans anyway. They didn't understand what it was like to be a Red Sox fan.

We then called various other family members—Joe's wife Lisa, my mom, my sister Ellen, and my sister Edie in Colorado. Edie's daughter Hayley checked in to make sure we were taking care of Papa, her grandfather. Everyone in the extended family was closely following our progress and wanted to know details. We felt sad that they couldn't be there to share the fun and take part in our adventure.

Just after noon, we reached Chickamauga, the site of the second deadliest battle of the Civil War. The battlefield was located in northwestern Georgia, just south of the Tennessee line, twenty miles southeast of Chattanooga.

In September 1863, the Union Army was intent on pushing the Confederates out of Tennessee and gaining complete control of Chattanooga's surroundings. Chattanooga was an important rail depot, at the time referred to as the "gateway to the South." The Confederates hoped to retake the city and force the Union Army north. After weeks of strategic maneuvering, the two sides met at Chickamauga. The number of troops involved was staggering with over 70,000 Union and 66,000 Confederate combatants.

Fighting began on September 19 and continued for over 48 hours, with only a short break at night. The terrain was mostly woods broken up by small meadows and occasional fields. There were intense artillery barrages from both sides and several hand-to-hand skirmishes. The wooded terrain, vast quantity of men, and inflated egos of several of the leaders made communication difficult. At times, confusion reigned. On the first day, the battle continued until long after dusk and poorly aimed bullets were as likely to kill friend as foe.

JKP's division was situated directly in the center of a two-mile line of combat. On the second day of fighting, the Union commander, General William S. Rosecrans acted upon erroneous intelligence that suggested the northern part of the Union line was faltering and needed reinforcements. He shifted some divisions from the middle of the line northward at the exact time his former West Point roommate, Confederate General James Longstreet, by luck more than anything else, staged an aggressive assault on the now depleted mid portion of the Union line. The Confederates broke through and split Union forces in two. The Johnnies captured private JKP Ferrell and 54 other members of the 51st OVI. The southern part of the Union line retreated, and the Confederates drove the northern flank back to Chattanooga.

In theory, the Confederates were victorious, the battlefield theirs to take. In truth, nobody won. Thirty-four thousand young men were dead, injured, missing, or captured. The fighting obliterated the landscape, entire forests reduced by artillery to stumps. Horse carcasses littered the killing field. Fellow countrymen fought one another, brutally maiming and killing, most without a clear understanding of what they were fighting for. Abraham Lincoln's brother-in-law, proudly fighting for the Confederate Army, died on the battlefield that day. Friend against friend, family member against family member.

We parked at the Visitor Center and slowly strolled toward the entrance. Using his walker, my dad moved deliberately, soaking in the sites. He stopped, looked over at me, and said, "So this is where our boy got captured. From here to Libby Prison in Richmond and then ultimately to Andersonville." He shook his head, I think contemplating the craziness of circumstances.

The battlefield stretched in all directions behind the welcome center. The grounds were well maintained, with several statues and monuments erected to commemorate the locations of different regiments. Inside the visitors' center, we watched a short film and talked to one of the park rangers who was very excited about JKP's story. He knew of Rosecrans' blunder, and he was sure that the OVI's capture was directly related. Their detachment was one of the only remaining units defending the thinned-out middle portion of the Union line. Longstreet's strike would have forced the men to pull back, and in the process, suffer casualties. The ranger gave us a map with directions to that part of the battlefield. The site was marked by a small monument dedicated to the 51st OVI.

After wandering among the exhibits in the welcome center, we made our way back to the motorhome and embarked on a slow seven mile "auto-tour" of the battlefield. We pulled over as we neared the area where the map marked the location of the 51st OVI. We found the monument in a clearing just off the road, next to dense woods. A large bronze relief plaque with an active battle scene was positioned within a stone frame and sat atop a bigger, rough-hewn, solid piece of granite. The monument stood ten to twelve feet high and, on the back, was a description of the OVI's movements during the battle with a list of casualties: 8 killed, 35 wounded, 55 captured or missing. I walked from the monument to the edge of the thick woods ten yards away. As I peered in between the trees, the others, including my dad holding onto Arlan's arm, came up behind me.

My dad gazed into the woods, smiled, and then called out "JKP, you in there?"

Conversation ceased as if we were expecting an answer. We heard the wind whistling through the leaves, birds chirping, and traffic noise from the road behind us. No reply from Ferrell. We walked back to the motorhome and continued the driving tour.

We briefly pulled over at a section of the battle site called Viniard Field and got out of the motorhome. A Park Ranger stood addressing a small group of visitors, and we walked over to listen. He told the story of the tranquil meadow that stretched behind him, the site of the bloodiest hand to hand combat at Chickamauga. Late on the second day of battle, Union Colonel John T. Wilder entered the clearing next to where we stood with his brigade of mounted infantry armed with seven-shot Spencer repeating rifles. Occupying most of the open field at that time was a large Confederate contingent of Texan infantry. Wilder's men mowed them down with a barrage of continuous rifle fire. Legend had it that by the end of that day, dead and dying bodies littered so much of the field that very little grass was visible; one could walk over bodies from one end to another without ever touching the ground.

The Ranger told us that Wilder himself was repulsed by the carnage, stating, "*It seemed a pity to kill men so. They fell in heaps, and I had it in my heart to order the firing to cease, to end the awful sight.*"

According to the Ranger, when night fell, groans and piercing wails of the dying filled the air, echoing from all directions. After two days of battle, the exhausted survivors tried to sleep through the haunting screams.

We were once again a somber bunch as we walked back to the motorhome, digesting all that we'd seen and heard. By 3:30 pm, we finished the driving tour and pulled out of Chickamauga.

CHAPTER 8
On to Stones River

Our next stop was Stones River National Battlefield in Murfrees-boro, Tennessee, the site of JKP's first capture, about 120 miles from our present location. As we headed northwest, we entered the central time zone and gained an hour. We hoped we'd make it to the battlefield before closing time. We were falling behind schedule.

We arrived at the battlefield entrance just after 4:30 pm to find its gate locked. We drove around the perimeter and noticed that residential and commercial development had squeezed this national landmark. In fact, only a small parcel of the original battlefield re-mained preserved. I asked David to check the atlas for nearby campgrounds. He directed me to Cedars of Lebanon State Park, the closest site, thirty miles due north. Shortly after leaving the battle-field we passed a homemade donut shop. We smelled the freshly baked pastry from the road as we drove by, and we unanimously agreed to make the donut shop the next day's breakfast stop.

Road Worthy

The park was a rugged pine forest with roads and trails cutting through hilly landscape. As we approached the entrance to the RV camping section, the gate was open. We pulled through, found a spot, and I carefully backed the motorhome between the pines. As I got out, I gazed upward and noticed two lumbering dead trees with their branches hanging over the RV. Amidst dense vegetation, there was just enough clearance around the passenger side to allow for a picnic table and firepit. We saw no other campers.

It was a pleasant evening, clear with a slight chill to the air. We grilled burgers outside, cooked some beans, and made a big salad. As dusk settled, we sat around the picnic table and enjoyed our dinner. For dessert, we indulged ourselves with frozen Snickers bars.

We cleaned up after dinner and then sat around the forward section of the RV and watched game five of the ALCS on our small television. Reception was good. At the end of six innings, the Yankees held a 4-2 lead. My skeptical traveling companions again began criticizing the Red Sox.

In the bottom of the eighth inning, the Red Sox tied it up. Neither team scored in the ninth, and the game went into extra innings.

As the four of us watched the later innings of the game, weather alerts started flashing across the television screen, first for severe thunderstorms, then for a tornado watch. Joe and I walked outside and found an almost full moon brightening the sky. There were no signs of harsh weather coming our way. As we continued watching the game, the warnings increased in frequency with maps showing the center of the storm passing directly over our location. We again walked outside and looked up; still, nothing ominous.

Arlan suggested we consider finding a campsite without two dead pine trees towering over us. The rest of us refused to acknowledge the warnings. It was too calm and peaceful outside.

Joe told him he needed to "man up," and I told him to "quit being such a mama's boy."

The game continued with both teams getting runners on base but neither side able to score. During the twelfth inning, a breeze began blowing outside our motorhome, gradually increasing in strength. We felt the temperature and barometric pressure dropping. The warning on our small television tracked continuously along the bottom of the screen, with descriptions of high winds, flooding rain, thunder, and lightning.

We again walked outside, my dad included, and looked up. Rapidly moving gray clouds migrating west to east, intermittently blocked out the moon and stars, replacing the previously clear night sky. We again examined the two dead pines and reconsidered Arlan's suggestion. My brother grudgingly admitted that Arlan might be right. If the forecast held, we didn't want to remain in our current location.

Arlan, Joe, David, and I set off with flashlights into the darkness to see if we could find a site without any external threats. A few spots away, we discovered an opening surrounded by brush and saplings but no tall trees. We ran back to our RV and disconnected from water and electric. I jumped into the driver's seat and fired up the engine. Under a pitch-black sky, I pulled forward onto the narrow dirt road and maneuvered up a hill and around a slight curve. Arlan and Joe walked in front of me. I pulled past the new site and then backed in, Joe on one side, Arlan on the other yelling directions. I centered the RV in the allotted space, no tall trees anywhere near. We resumed watching the game.

In the bottom of the fourteenth inning, with one out, Johnny Damon came to the plate. My father looked over at me, slowly shaking his head. The pitcher got behind in the count, and Damon ended up walking. After an easy out, Manny Ramirez took a ball that was just millimeters outside the strike zone on a 3-2 count. With two outs, David Ortiz came to the plate with Damon on second and Ramirez on first.

Ortiz had already hit two homers, but he was not finished. He smacked a fastball into center field, and Damon, hair flying as he ran, easily scored from second base to win the game. I looked over at my father and slowly nodded my head with a victorious (and somewhat smug) grin on my face. The series now stood 3-2, still in favor of the Yankees, but the Red Sox were back in it. I sensed the team and their fans were starting to believe. Nobody around me was convinced, but I knew Joy had watched the game and that she'd be going to bed with newfound confidence that our boys might pull this series out.

The game lasted six hours, and it was past 11 pm when we settled into our sleeping spots and turned out the lights. The wind was now steady, and rain began to fall. It was calming, almost hypnotic, and the five of us instantly fell asleep.

About an hour later, we caught the brunt of the storm. Wind-blown rain pelted our motorhome, creating a constant pounding. I awakened and heard the wind howling over the driving rain. Arlan was snoring, oblivious to the cacophony of water hitting metal and wind shaking our flimsy siding, but everyone else was awake. Above the din, It was impossible to talk to one another.

I felt like I was Dorothy in the Wizard of Oz as her house spun in the vortex of a tornado. I nervously awaited our blast off. And then the rain slowed, and the wind abated. I felt relieved, falsely thinking that we were through the worst part of the storm. A few minutes later, lightning started flashing around us followed by crashes of thunder. The flashes got closer and closer to one another, and the booms of thunder louder and louder. The wind picked back up and then pounding rain resumed. I curled up in my sleeping bag and closed my eyes, trying to ignore the terrifying exhibition of nature's wrath. Afraid our motorhome was going to fall victim to the furious storm, I prayed for the lightning and thunder to stop.

I eventually dozed off and started dreaming. I was lying on my abdomen in the woods. The storm raged around me, and I was cold and wet. And then I felt terror consume me as I realized the flashes and booms were not from a storm but from mortars and shells, lobbed at me by an adversary that wanted to eviscerate me. I could feel my enemy close by. Then I saw shapes outlined by flashes of exploding bombs, bayonets drawn, closing in. I wanted to run, but I couldn't move. There was nowhere to go. And then I awakened, my heart racing. My dream seemed so real that I wondered if I had temporarily travelled back to a Civil War battlefield. Did I just witness Ferrell's first capture? Get a taste for how he felt? The storm continued outside. I felt relieved, secure and warm in my cramped quarters. I thought about Joy and our two daughters back in Rhode Island. Though shaken by my nightmare, I eventually fell back asleep.

We awakened Tuesday morning around 8 am. All of us, except Arlan, were exhausted from the night's events. We drank a few cups of coffee and then gathered our gear. We took a quick walk to view our previous campsite, my dad between Joe and Arlan, holding onto their arms. The two large pines, though still standing, had shed several thick branches onto the RV site below. We were lucky we had moved.

By 9 am, we were heading back toward Stones River Battlefield. Aside from puddles everywhere, there were no signs of the violent storm that had blown through a few hours earlier. In its wake, clear skies and cool, dry air. As we drove southward, our spirits lifted, and we looked forward to continuing our adventure. We were also excited about the fresh-baked donuts we anticipated for breakfast. Sometimes it does not take much to restore the zeal of five average, overtired guys on a journey of discovery.

We rehashed the details of the previous night's endless lightning display. Joe referred to it as the "perfect storm." Though better rested than the other four of us, after hearing our descriptions, Arlan regretted missing the commotion. We wondered aloud what it would have been like for JKP to have endured such a night, alone in a wet tent with no warning and little protection. I told the others about my dream. My dad felt sure that JKP was reaching out to us, offering a glimpse of Civil War fighting, channeling some of his intense fears and emotions from a century-and-a-half earlier. I shuddered as I remembered the dread of enemy soldiers bearing down on me with bayonets drawn.

The smell and taste of homemade donuts erased all memories of the night before. The five of us consumed two dozen and washed them down with freshly brewed coffee. It wasn't the healthiest breakfast, but it was certainly very satisfying.

I had attempted to research the Battle of Stone's River, and the more I read, the more confused I got. Miscommunication, uncertainty, and poorly understood objectives characterized most of the major Civil War battles, this one included. No one wanted to give the order to attack for fear that someone higher in rank would question or criticize the decision, especially if the outcome was defeat. So, there was continuous troop maneuvering, and then suddenly fierce and close-handed engagement, sometimes unplanned.

The two sides fought this battle over four days in the dead of winter, in freezing rain over rough terrain. The casualty rate was very high: 30% of the 80,000 combatants killed, injured, missing, or captured. In the end, Union leaders declared it a Yank victory, though anyone who objectively researched the battle would conclude that there was no clear winner.

We walked into the reception center and discussed the battle with one of the curators. He was very interested in our story about JKP and directed us to a map that showed the different locations of infantry divisions. The preserved portion of battlefield was much smaller than the original with modern civilization encroaching on all sides. It was hard to escape the present with sounds of suburbia surrounding us.

We took a quick driving tour of the national site but did not find the exact spot where the Rebels had captured JKP. We again spied a park ranger addressing a group of tourists and parked the motorhome and walked over to learn more.

The ranger described one very poignant moment before battle. As evening merged into night on December 31, 1862, the two sides formed their lines, in some places no more than a hundred yards apart. Different regimental bands began playing songs. At first, the different bands competed with one another. When one band struck up the favorite Civil War ballad *Home Sweet Home,* bands on both sides of the battlefield joined in and all the soldiers, Union and Confederate, sang as a single chorus. For a brief period of time, the men forgot their differences and thought of their families back home, their common bond.

"Mid pleasures and palaces
Though I may roam
Be it ever so humble
There's no place like home
A charm from the sky
Seems to hallow us there
Which seek thro' the world
Is ne'er met with elsewhere

Home! Home!
Sweet, sweet, home!
There's no place like home
There's no place like home

To thee I'll return
Overburdened with care
The heart's dearest solace
Will smile on me there

No more from that cottage
Again I will roam
Be it ever so humble
There's no place like home

Home! Home!
Sweet sweet home
There's no place like home
There's no place like home"

And then the song ended, instruments and voices quieted. The soldiers, boys and men alike, lay on the frigid ground, scared and longing for home. Some probably contemplated the irony that many of the faceless voices carried plaintively over the breeze that evening belonged to soldiers they would engage and possibly kill in the morning. Because of the obstinacy and irrationality of the human condition, the inability to work out differences, and because they were told to do so, they would continue savagely killing their own countrymen until one side was soundly defeated and forced to concede. Thousands of men, who for one brief moment sang in unison, would die at the hands of each other and never return to their earthly homes.

CHAPTER 9
On to the Buckeye State

By noon we were ready to continue onward. Our plan for the afternoon was to get as close as possible to Uhrichsville, Ferrell's hometown. We passed through northern Tennessee into Kentucky heading towards Louisville.

As we progressed further north, the fall colors became more dramatic. My family members, all Floridians, were awed by the vibrant palate of autumn in the north. The air was crisp and the sky blue with occasional wispy clouds. For much of the afternoon, my traveling companions gazed out the windows, occasionally commenting on some passing natural beauty. They also intermittently dozed off. We ate a late lunch as we drove, finishing off the salami, cheese, chips, and apples. We were running low on food.

We reached Louisville and continued northeast toward Ohio. We stopped once for gas and then crossed the Ohio River into Cincinnati at around 5 pm. Traffic was surprisingly light, with no delays motoring through downtown Cincinnati. About an hour north, as dusk hit, I asked David if he could find a suitable spot to stop for the night. He examined the atlas and suggested Buckeye Lake Campground, just east of Columbus and less than an hour from our present location. As the sun set, increasing fog limited visibility. I was happy to exit the interstate.

As we neared our camping destination, we decided we should stock up on food. We saw a neon light for Kroger and pulled into the parking lot. After seven hours of sitting, we were happy to get outside and stretch our legs. The night air was chilly, and we put on sweatshirts or jackets. The fabulous five led by my dad in the middle pushing his walker with two of us on each side as his wing-men, slowly marched through the mist, across the asphalt to the store's entrance. I felt like I was in an old western or maybe medieval England, part of a band of merry men on a worthy mission in the middle of God knows where, seeking the truth about a long-forgotten war hero. We were battle-tested, a bit road weary, unshaven, and looking a little rough.

Once inside the grocery store, we grabbed two carts, and the five of us stayed together as we traversed every aisle, haphazardly grabbing items and replenishing our food stores. We approached the check-out line, and Arlan took out his wallet and offered to pay. The rest of us bagged items and filled the carts. We then made our way back through the mist to our motorhome, my dad again in the lead, two of us pushing shopping carts trailing behind him.

The campground was only a few miles up the road, and as we pulled into the entrance we passed a small, brightly lit, cabin-like structure. The owner sat inside finishing the day's business. He cheerfully welcomed us, checked us in, and then personally escorted us to our site. We told him the story of our journey as he helped hook up our electric and water lines. He listened intently, and it seemed as if he hoped we would invite him to join us. And then it hit me.

We were in Ohio, the heart of the Midwest, the state where I was born. People here took time to listen and expressed genuine interest.

After we were situated, the owner left promising to return in the morning to check on us. We stowed our newly purchased food and then cooked dinner. After eating, we turned on game six of the ALCS. Reception was excellent.

Game six was back in New York. That was the bad news. The good news was that Curt Schilling, Boston's ace, was the starting pitcher for the Sox. We began watching at the end of the third inning, just in time to see Boston score four runs. The Red Sox never looked back, with Schilling pitching an outstanding game, allowing only four hits over seven innings. The final score was 4-2. Boston had become the first team in history to force a game seven in a playoff series after being down 3-0.

Our group was exhausted; the others had retired before the game ended. As I celebrated by myself in silence, I looked to the rear of the motorhome. Arlan and David were tightly packed in the bed to my right with Joe sprawled out on the smaller bed to my left. Just as I was about to turn off the small forward light and climb between the seats to my berth on the floor, my dad exited the bathroom and slowly limped to his cozy quarters in the far rear. He pushed open the door to his suite and stood hunched over the edge of his bed. Before he plopped down onto the welcoming mattress, he looked back over his shoulder and his eyes caught mine. In the semi-darkness, I saw a smile slowly form on his weary face. I smiled back and gave him a quick salute.

I hesitated for a second, perched on the front seat as a I watched him turn and collapse onto his bed. I considered this giant of a man, my father, beaten down by age and infirmity but still thrilled to be off with the guys on another adventure. I felt a momentary pang of guilt for allowing our lives to become so separated. I thought back to the "disconnect" between us that seemed to peak during my high school and college years. Was it my fault? A long-forgotten memory of the two of us in synchrony suddenly flashed into my mind. I smiled and thought to myself, maybe the void between us was not as profound as I remembered.

Back in May 1980, after I graduated from college, I drove my Chevy Biscayne from Atlanta to my home in Deerfield Beach. I arrived in South Florida on a Sunday evening, exhausted from graduation, a week of partying, and the day's twelve-hour drive. As soon as I walked through the front door, my dad bolted out to greet me.

"Hey, you wanna go to Europe with me for a week or two?"

Surprised, I responded, "Sure. When do you want to go and how are we getting there?"

My dad replied, "There's this new, budget airline flying out of Miami. You can't make a reservation. Instead, you call and order a ticket, and then your name goes on a list. They contact you a few days ahead of departure. So, we might leave tomorrow, or we might leave two weeks from now. If you're in, I'll call and reserve two tickets."

I interrupted him. "Where are we going to stay?"

He smiled. "I thought we could stay with the Schmidts in Garmisch-Partenkirchen, Germany. We can get away from the heat and hang out in the Bavarian Alps. The tickets are really cheap."

My family had met the Schmidts on a previous family trip to Europe, one that I had missed. Mr. Schmidt was the schoolmaster in Garmisch. He and his wife had three boys, twins who were a couple of years younger than me and a third son my brother's age. One of the twins had visited and lived with my family while I was away at college. He had hoped to improve his tennis game and take classes at Deerfield Beach High School. It turned out that he hated Florida, especially the suffocating late summer heat and humidity. He lasted only a few weeks, but my parents remained close friends with his parents after he left, exchanging holiday cards and occasional letters. The Schmidts lived in a spacious chalet on the outskirts of downtown Garmisch, and they were gracious hosts who enjoyed having guests.

I gave my dad the thumbs up. What the hell! I could avoid finding a job for a few weeks and hopefully drink some good German beer. My dad secured a reservation, and two days later we flew to London and then caught a train to Munich. Mr. Schmidt met us in Munich, and I remember the enthralling ride in his spacious Mercedes sedan through the mountains of southern Germany to their home in Garmisch.

The whole Schmidt family was home for the summer. The twins, now twenty years old, and their close friends had recently developed a passion for basketball. They had a key to the high school gym, which was about 75% the length of an American high school basketball court with old wooden backboards bracketed to the walls on both ends. For the first few nights, as my dad sat and had tea with Mr. and Mrs. Schmidt after dinner, I left with a small group of German guys to play basketball. My new German friends were very athletic and most of them were taller than me, easily able to dunk. They knew the rules of the game and what they were supposed to do. But they were relative novices, and no matter the amount of athleticism, basketball is not a game that can be mastered in a few months.

Our third or fourth evening, while my dad and I were enjoying dinner with our hosts and some of their friends, the twins very directly challenged us to a two-on-two basketball game.

I was finishing a stein of Lowenbrau, a bit surprised at their bluntness but feeling brave. I looked at my dad and then back at the twins and replied, "You will need at least two other players to beat the two of us."

They didn't argue. "Okay, we will get two friends and play you two tomorrow night in the school gym: four on two; full court."

I was happy about playing full court because it would give me room to maneuver and avoid getting caged by four defenders. My dad was not a basketball player; I foresaw his role as mostly assisting defensively, rebounding, and then getting the ball out quickly so I could take off one on four.

My dad was excited to be part of the challenge. This was before any of his chronic ailments had set in, and he could still move pretty well. I looked over at Mr. and Mrs. Schmidt. They seemed a bit uncomfortable, afraid that their sons had sounded confrontational. Mrs. Schmidt broke the uneasy silence. She smiled and said, "We will come and watch."

The youngest Schmidt, who had been practicing English since our arrival, jumped up. "I cannot wait to see one player and an old guy beat my brothers and their friends. I will tell everyone!"

The next evening, before dinner, we walked to the high school gym, the entire Schmidt family and several of the twins' friends. We grabbed a few good balls, and my father and I went to one end of the gym to warm up while the team of four assembled on the other end. I was feeling "ready."

I huddled with my dad and noticed the look of determination on his face. I whispered, "Okay, we will play a 1-1 zone with you under the basket and me chasing the ball. These guys can't shoot, so if we don't give them lay-ups, we should be able to limit their scoring. If they do score, get the ball inbounds quickly, so they don't have time to set up. These four guys can't stop us. We will run them into the ground."

The twins and their two friends met my dad and me at half court. I spoke to the group. "Okay, you guys know the rules. Players call their own fouls and no arguing if someone makes a call. First team to fifteen baskets wins. You can sub in if the other guys want to play."

Everyone nodded heads in agreement. Because we were guests, we got the ball first.

It took us only twenty minutes to defeat the young German players. My dad stuck to the game plan, and I took off on every rebound or inbounds pass. They gave me nothing close to the rim, but

I killed them with fifteen to twenty footers. The last point to win the game was epic.

My father rebounded a missed shot and shoved a pass out to me. Most of the time, he stayed on the defensive end of the court, conserving his energy. The four Germans turned their attention to me as I streaked up the right side of the court, three of them in front of me, one trailing, no one focused on my father. My dad knew that I was not going to get anything easy for the last point. Out of the corner of my eye, I saw him trailing play. I continued down to the right corner, all four of them within a few feet of me. As I pulled up my dribble and left my feet, initially planning on a desperate jump shot from the corner, I saw my dad wide open at the top of the key. Instead of shooting, I whizzed a pass to my father who took one dribble and drilled a jump shot from the foul line. No arch. Straight through the basket. Game over.

My dad was so excited he raced over to me and gave me a high five. We looked over at the four dejected Germans and said, "Maybe next time boys."

The clarity of the above remembrance was so intense that it startled me. I hadn't thought about that game for decades, but I remembered it perfectly now. I could almost smell the small gym, sense my father's excitement, and see that glorious final shot.

I climbed into my sleeping bag and before closing my eyes, I whispered to myself, "Dad, how 'bout the time we kicked the German kids' asses?"

We awoke the next morning before 8 am to overcast skies and an outdoor temperature in the mid-fifties. It was still foggy with a low-lying mist. The surrounding trees wore coats of autumn colors. We took an unhurried walk through the campground, but despite our collective efforts, we did not find any buckeyes. For those non-Midwesterners reading this, the buckeye tree is the state tree of Ohio, and buckeyes are the nuts dropped by the tree. They are hard, smooth, and deep brown in color, about three quarters the size of an egg—another striking example of nature's beauty and craftsmanship.

We made our way back to the motorhome and began working on breakfast, which pitted Joe making spiced up eggs and bacon outside against David making pancakes inside in a gourmet cooking contest. David protected his cooking space, afraid we might discover his "special" pancake recipe. My father, Arlan, and I were happy to get out of their way and be the judges (and beneficiaries) of their cooking efforts. We sat outside at a picnic table drinking coffee as we watched the two of them work. Not only did they cook, they cut up fruit, set the table, and refilled our coffee cups.

I sensed my dad felt a little strange, maybe nostalgic, being back in Ohio. But he also seemed content. He was very excited at the prospect of revisiting Union Cemetery in Uhrichsville and finding JKP's grave. He was a little miffed at me for making the executive decision to bypass The Dayton Air Museum, a place he had always wanted to visit, but there was no way to work it into our remaining timeframe. We still had a lot of ground to cover, and I had to get the RV back to Fort Lauderdale by noon on Saturday, now only three days away, and then fly back to Rhode Island early the following morning.

The culinary efforts of Joe and David resulted in a superb breakfast. All five of us had seconds and then thirds. As we were finishing, the friendly campground owner arrived. He ate the last remaining pancake.

We cleaned up and readied the motorhome for departure. We waved good-by to our new friend as we exited the campground. I drove, retracing our route from the previous night for a few miles before merging onto the interstate.

CHAPTER 10
Uhrichsville

Tom Hamilton, the genealogist who had helped my father piece together JKP's life story, died unexpectedly from a heart attack two months before our trip. My father was very saddened by Tom's sudden passing as the two of them had become close long-distance pen pals and friends. He had contacted Tom's wife Mary in August to offer condolences. He told her that he (we) would stop by for a short visit when we passed through Uhrichsville in the fall. As we continued eastward on I-70, my father called Mary by cell phone. She said she could meet us that evening and provided directions to her home.

As we drove, the light fog lifted, and the sky cleared. By the time we got off the interstate onto Route 36 toward Uhrichsville, it was another classic fall day, the blue sky interrupted sporadically by slowly drifting clouds. The colors of nature flashed by, accentuated by the bright sun and cool, dry air. We passed through a valley with low lying hills on both sides and emerged into Uhrichsville proper. We exited Route 36 in town onto Water Street heading south.

Urhichsville had a feel of small town, blue collar, working-class mid-America. It was clean with scattered businesses but no visible national chains. The houses were well-kept, some small, some large, but nothing fancy. The streets were mostly empty, though a few of the residents were taking advantage of the bright fall day, walking the gently sloping streets, or riding their bicycles. Nobody seemed to be in a hurry.

When we found Union Cemetery, I carefully maneuvered our RV through the gate and then pulled over, partly onto the grass. I turned the engine off, and we sat for a few moments looking at one another. After months of discussion and hours of planning, we had arrived at our final destination. We were excited, but also a bit sad that our long journey was near completion. Our moment to find Ferrell's final resting place and honor him was at hand.

The graveyard was huge, stretching far into the distance on all sides especially to the north. Beyond the boundaries of the cemetery, there was a golf course and beyond the golf course, gently rolling hills dressed in fall colors. We gazed out at thousands of gravestones, some big and some small in different states of wear and disrepair. Pines and big shade trees dotted the grounds. We realized that if the five of us started off randomly in different directions, it might still take all day to find JKP's gravestone.

It was late morning when we stepped outside the motorhome. It felt like autumn, with the temperature in the low sixties and increasing as the sun continued its climb. The air was clean, and there was a satisfying smell of fallen leaves and cut grass. My father hoped we would find David Aldergate, the supervisor of the cemetery he had communicated with ten months earlier.

We walked on the paved road deeper into the cemetery. We came to a circle where the road did a complete 360, with two points of egress off the circle. In the middle of the circle, surrounded by a three-foot-high, black, wrought iron fence stood an intricately designed monument dedicated to local residents who had fought and died during the Civil War. The monument was made from limestone and consisted of a tree sheared off about twenty feet above the ground, presumably by shelling from artillery. A dead branch hung limply off the remaining trunk. At the base of the tree, a proud, stoic Union soldier stood upright, leaning slightly against his gun, which was perpendicular to the ground. He was holding his canteen, unscrewing the top. About ten feet in front of him, lying on the ground, was a second soldier, wounded, looking back at the first soldier, pleading, perhaps for water. The wounded soldier looked to be a Confederate. Scattered around the tree were exposed roots, some rocks, and a broken wagon wheel, part of its rim and spokes missing.

We couldn't help but think that this monument perfectly embodied the essence of the Civil War, the Union beating and breaking its brother but then offering a helping hand to rebuild and reunite. The striking detail of the sculpture, its genius and symbolism, stunned us. The five of us stared at it in silence.

Just ahead, off the first exit road from the circle, we saw a rectangular, one-story stone building. We ambled toward it thinking it might be the caretaker's office. On the far end was a door marked "Entrance." We opened it and walked into a small office. Behind an old wooden desk sat a rotund man who looked to be in his thirties. He had a cheerful face, and he stood up, smiled, and asked, "What can I do for you?"

My father briefly recounted the story of the mallet and expressed our hope of finding JKP's grave. He asked if David Aldergate was working.

The man replied, "No. David is off today." He walked around the desk and extended his hand. "My name is John Chapman. I'm happy to help you."

We introduced ourselves, and my father sat down in a chair next to John's desk.

John asked us "When did Mr. Ferrell die?"

My dad answered, "1929." He continued, "David Aldergate told me that JKP was buried in section B. Do you know where that is?"

John replied, "Section B includes the original cemetery confines before it was enlarged. It's still a very large area. Let's find Ferrell's file, and we should be able to narrow it down a bit. You said 1929?"

My dad nodded.

John stood up, went into a back room, and returned with a large, dusty register labeled "1929." He flipped through the pages, carefully looking down at the list of names. My dad sat next to him and stared intently at the pages.

The other four of us walked outside and randomly roamed among the gravestones. I headed back to the Civil War monument and slowly circled its perimeter to see if Ferrell's name was on any of the plaques that hung off the sturdy wrought iron fencing. I also searched the graves nearby, deducing that Ferrell's might be in proximity, in this section clearly dedicated to the Civil War. No luck.

I walked back to the building. My dad was still inside. John was giving him information from the graveyard registry about next of kin, my father writing it all down in the little pocket notepad he had brought on the trip.

I asked John, "Does lot 66 narrow things down at all? David Aldergate told my dad section B, lot 66."

John replied, "It means nothing to me, but let's see if we can find an old map that might help." He disappeared into the back room filled with old records.

By now, it was just past noon. I walked outside and made my way over to Joe, Arlan, and David. They continued fanning out from the main road and had traveled 300 yards from the motorhome and about 100 yards from the caretaker's cottage. It was warm outside, and several people had entered the cemetery, walking or riding

113

bikes. It seemed that it was a popular destination at the noon hour for locals on their lunch breaks.

The four of us looked back at the caretaker's office and saw my father and John Chapman emerge. They waved us over. When we assembled around the two of them, John exclaimed, "As best I can tell, your man should be buried about a quarter mile up the road on the left."

I asked John, "Are there any Ferrells still residing in town?"

John shook his head. "Not that I know of, but there is an elderly gentleman in his eighties, Charlie, who will be riding his bike through here any minute. He knows everyone in town. If you see an older guy riding a three-wheeler, ask him."

John continued, "I have to go eat my lunch, but I'll catch up with you guys later and see how you are making out."

The five of us started up the road to the area John had suggested. About 400 yards to the north, we again fanned out over the grass to the left, carefully walking along the rows of graves. Most of the townspeople who saw us came over to see what we were looking for. When we told them, each interrupted his or her walk to help us search. At the height of the lunch hour, we had a large contingent of congenial Midwesterners looking for JKP's grave.

At around 12:45 pm, I noticed a refined, elderly gentleman slowly making his way toward us, pedaling a three-wheeler on the main cemetery road. I jogged back to intercept him. As he came abreast, he stopped, aware that I wanted to talk.

"Charlie?" I asked.

"At your service, young man. What can I do for you?"

I replied, "We are looking for a Civil War soldier's grave, and…"

He interrupted me, "You and half the town it seems."

"Well, yes sir. Your townspeople have extended their assistance. It seems like a very friendly place."

"Yes, it certainly is," he emphasized. "During World War II, we were known as America's hometown. Do you know the story of the rail depot?"

I shook my head. "No."

Charlie continued. "During World War II, many soldiers going off to war passed through our railroad depot heading to either coast to embark for the European or Pacific theatres. The townspeople of Uhrichsville noted the forlorn looks on the faces of those boys staring out the windows of loaded trains. The women of the area banded together and formed a canteen. Every train going through our town stopped and had a short break for the soldiers to mingle with the town-folk and enjoy a large, hot, home-cooked meal. Our town's goal was to send each boy, regardless of point of origin, skin color, religion, etc. off with a smile. So yes, we have a history of being a friendly town. Now how can I help you?"

I answered, "Well, the name of our Civil War hero is JKP Ferrell. John Chapman told us to ask if you know of this individual. We were also curious as to whether any Ferrells still lived in town."

Charlie rubbed his forehead and then his chin. His brow wrinkled as he considered my questions. "I do recall that there were some Ferrells living in town when I was a young boy. One family lived in a big white house just off Main Street. I vaguely remember that name held in high esteem, perhaps because of ancestors who fought admirably during the Civil War. But I have not heard that name in decades, and I'm not sure if any family members are left in town."

He went on, "I assume that's your motorhome I passed with the Florida plates? How are you related to this Ferrell fellow?"

I briefly told Charlie the story about the mallet and what we knew about JKP's service during the Civil War including his stay at Andersonville.

115

Charlie climbed back onto his bike seat nodding his head as he listened to my story. "Andersonville—nothing good about that place."

When he was situated on his seat and had his feet on the pedals, he looked up at me. "Well, I wish you good luck in your quest. I'm glad you got to visit our little town. Now I best continue my journey and get home or my wife will send the police looking for me."

I looked back at the small group of individuals snaking among the graves. The crowd had thinned, people abandoning the hunt to return to work. I noticed my dad conversing with an attractive young woman in her twenties or early thirties. I walked toward them and noticed that my dad looked frustrated, I think because traversing the rolling grass between graves was very difficult with his walker. Before I reached them, the woman extended her arm. My father grabbed it, and the two of them slowly edged off the pavement onto the grass and back amidst the graves, my father ditching the walker. With a big smile on his face, he looked back at me and winked.

I'm not sure how long we continued searching or who found the grave, but in the mid to late afternoon, as the sun was moving westward, we entered an area of the graveyard with small pine trees and scattered large maples. By now, it was just the five of us. John Chapman had come out of his office to check our progress a few times during the afternoon, but after he finished his office hours, he left for home. Several others had also come and gone over the course of the day.

About twenty feet in front of two maples we found an upright piece of smoothly polished, engraved, white granite sitting atop a rough-hewn rectangular base. The combined pieces stood four to five feet off the ground. On the front was inscribed FERRELL. John Chapman had told us that he thought we'd find a Ferrell plot that still had empty spaces. About ten to fifteen feet directly in front of the upright family monument, we found two side by side, small, rectangular pieces of granite standing ten to twelve inches above the grass. On the top of one, etched into the stone:

GRANDFATHER
JOHN K. P. FERRELL
AUG. 16, 1844
FEB 4, 1929
CO. A. 61ST REG O.V.I.

The other rectangular marker stood in line with the first a few feet over:

GRANDMOTHER
LYDIA MARGREAT
DEC. 27, 1847
MARCH 6, 1928

As I gazed down at the two grave markers with my four traveling companions gathered around me, several thoughts passed through my mind. Despite his Civil War experiences including an extended incarceration as a POW at Andersonville, JKP had gone on to lead a long life—eighty-five years. He had outlived his wife and his daughter. I was a bit miffed that the grave marker was in error about his Civil War service. Suspecting that JKP held great pride in being part of the 51st OVI, I strongly felt that the error needed to be corrected, the six changed to a five, though it was clearly not up to me. I wondered if others over the years had noticed and been equally annoyed.

I also couldn't take my eyes off of "GRANDFATHER." Despite obvious pride in his wartime service and great passion for the Grand Army of the Republic, JKP's most enduring legacy, as dictated by him and/or his extended family members seemed to be as the patriarch of his family. In the end and for eternity, this is what best defined him.

GRANDFATHER. Love of country, but foremost, love of family. No wonder my dad felt like such a kindred spirit. And then I realized that we had uncovered only a small bit of knowledge about Ferrell's life. What felt so compelling to us about his story—his military service, imprisonment, and ultimate release—was likely not nearly as important to him as his family, friends, this town, or the mundane, day-to-day moments that shaped his life. From my father's research and our trip, we got a cursory glimpse into JKP's past. In truth we knew very few of the vital details that defined his life. And so it is with history; it's impossible to know more.

I glanced back at the others, all of them staring at the ground, lost in thought. My dad looked up and suggested we get the motorhome, drive back, and pay our final respects. He had purchased flowers the night before at Kroger, and he wanted to leave them on the grave. We took pictures and recorded some video. I told the others that I would run back and get the RV. Joe offered to go with me, and we half walked, half jogged the mile or so to the motorhome and then drove it back. I grabbed the flowers, and Joe and I rejoined the others.

As we stood over JKP's grave, the sun continued its descent. It was pre-dusk, and there was a slight chill to the air. My dad looked over at the four of us and said, "I think everyone should say a few words."

He proceeded to lay the flowers over the small tombstone, and with a furled brow and a few tears in his eyes, he thanked JKP—for his service, for the life he lived afterwards, for making the mallet, for leading my father to it, and for bringing us together on such a remarkable journey of discovery. My dad had forged an intense connection with JKP, his show of emotion arising out of respect, love, and gratitude. When finished speaking, he carefully stepped back from the grave marker.

My dad asked David to go next. David approached JKP's gravestone, and with a solemn look on his face, stood there for a few minutes, speechless. He looked up at the sky and then over at the rest of us, and finally back down at the ground. In a slow, deliberate tone, he said, "He was a good guy." He then slowly stepped back to where the rest of us stood.

I think partly because of the intensity of the moment, Joe, Arlan, and I got a wicked case of the giggles over David's simple, concise summation. We purposely avoided eye contact with each other, coughing and clearing our throats to hide our laughter, trying to stay out of my father's direct line of vision. We meant nothing disrespectful to JKP. I guess it was one of those nervous things, a kind of emotional release. And when the three of us started laughing, sometimes it was impossible to stop. None of us could compose himself long enough to follow David's short oratory, and after several minutes of silence, broken only by fake coughs and other odd vocalizations made trying to cover our chortles, my dad asked, "Does anyone else want to say something?"

Thankfully, the shade trees and long shadows made it difficult to see very well, and the sounds of crickets and songbirds drowned out Arlan's occasional snicker and Joe's and my responding snorts and grunts.

Arlan collected himself and took a few steps forward. "David said it all. I don't think there's anything else to say."

I said, "Here, here."

Joe said, "Desh Raight."

My dad seemed satisfied with that, and we officially ended our ceremony. We stood there looking at one another for a few minutes and then made our way back to the motorhome. We climbed in and slowly followed the road through the rest of Union Cemetery and back into town.

It was almost completely dark as we headed to Water Street and made our way to Mary Hamilton's small home. We parked the

RV a block away, in front of the high school. There were "no parking" signs everywhere, so we left David with our vehicle, the other four of us assembling outside, my father with his walker. We heard the high school band practicing and an occasional whistle blowing in the distance as coaches directed drills on the football field behind the high school.

When we knocked on Mary's door, she immediately opened it and invited us in. We sat in her small living room and offered our condolences over Tom's passing. My dad said a few complimentary things about her husband and handed her a bouquet of flowers and a copy of his published article about JKP. We then got up, each gave Mary a hug, and bid her farewell.

As we walked back to the motorhome, we passed a short but muscular kid with a gruff face in full football pads carrying his helmet. He seemed oblivious as he walked toward us in full stride. My dad caught his eye and asked, "What position do you play?"

The teenager slowed and then stopped. He looked back at us, not smiling and not frowning. He answered, "Guard."

My father asked, "Right or left?"

"Left," he replied curtly.

My dad retorted, "You any good?"

He stared my father down, and with no hesitation he nodded his head and said, "Yes, I am." He then continued on his way.

We made our way back to the motorhome, my dad very deliberately pushing his walker, deep in thought, probably traveling back to a time when he walked in that young man's shoes, filled with confidence, his whole life ahead of him.

CHAPTER 11
Closing It Out

hen we reached the RV, I fired up the engine and looked
back at the others. My dad wanted to explore the railroad
museum in Dennison, Uhrichsville's twin city, but the museum had closed for the day, which meant we would have to spend
the night nearby, visit in the morning, and then start our trip south
sometime after noon the following day. We still had 24 hours of hard
driving between us and home and only two days left to do it. I was
worried that any minor problem might set us back, so I suggested
we start home. We would make the Dennison Rail Museum a priority on our next trip, which we were already starting to plan. My dad
was disappointed, but he deferred to me.

Heading home felt bittersweet. We had accomplished our
goals. I was anxious to get back to my family, but I knew I would
miss the excitement of traveling and the connection the five of us
had established over the past five days. It's always fun visiting

unfamiliar places, not knowing what to expect; it's inevitably sad when a good trip comes to an end and its participants go their separate ways. I knew I would miss the other four guys.

As we motored southward, the weather changed, and we encountered intermittent light drizzle, low lying fog, and a few hard rains. Still, we made good time through southern Ohio onto the West Virginia Turnpike. In West Virginia, the trucking traffic was especially heavy, and large semi's continuously roared past us. We were a tired bunch, and my father nodded off a few times. We passed snacks around and made a plan to enjoy a late dinner once we found a spot to park our RV for the night.

South of Charleston, I began to tire. I asked David if there were any campgrounds ahead. He turned on the interior light and studied the atlas. He found a state park called Camp Creek that advertised RV sites, thirty miles from our present location.

A half hour later, we turned off the highway, found the park's entrance, and made our way through the darkness to the camping area. When we reached the RV section, there was no one around, but the gate was open. We entered and drove down a rugged dirt road into a large circle. We found a level space next to a fast flowing, narrow river. With Joe and Arlan directing me, I carefully backed in.

I looked forward to game seven of the ALCS, which I knew had already started. I turned on our little television and channel surfed. Joe fired up his portable gas grill outside, and Arlan lit the stove inside. A late-night dinner of grilled hot dogs and baked beans, our staple on this trip, followed. I found the game. Reception was surprisingly good considering we seemed to be in the middle of nowhere. My father joined me up front as Joe called from outside to inform us that the scenery was "wicked cool…like Colorado, man."

It was still only the top of the second inning, and Boston had the bases loaded and held a 2-0 lead. Johnny Damon was batting. The broadcaster announced that Damon was only 3 of 29 coming into tonight's game. He had hit safely in the first inning, but then the Yankees threw him out at the plate. My dad was about to make a comment just as the pitcher went into his motion and threw to the plate. SMACK!!! Damon connected, full on, and the Yankees' crowd went silent as the ball sailed out of the park. A grand-slam home run in the deciding game. Damon had redeemed himself. Two innings later he hit a two-run homer, and the Red Sox never looked back, winning game seven handily. Against all odds, they had come back and won four straight games to steal the series. The Sox had finally broken the "Curse of the Bambino."

After the long eventful day, we were exhausted by the end of the game. We fell asleep within minutes.

We woke up the next morning after 9 am. We felt no urgency. We had no schedule to keep, select points of interest to visit, or itinerary to follow. We were on cruise control, five dudes, heading home.

David brewed coffee as the rest of us slowly shed our sleeping bags, sat up, and eventually dressed. It was cloudy outside with rain threatening. We put on a few layers, and when the coffee was ready, we each poured a cup and descended the metal steps of the motorhome to a picnic table sitting next to the churning river. Between the temperature and the cold surrounding mist, it felt raw. But the surroundings were spectacular—low mountains bathed in fall colors with rocky outcroppings hanging over the boiling river. It was quiet and peaceful. My dad was the last to join us. When he pushed open the door of the motorhome, all four of us jumped up to help him down the steps and seat him at the table. David offered him a cup of hot coffee.

I couldn't help but chide my father. "How 'bout those Red Sox? Did Johnny Damon come through in a big way or what?"

My dad grumbled a few incoherent words, and then he looked at me and smiled. "Okay, you were right."

After a quick breakfast, we explored the camping area. Scattered everywhere on the ground, we found the motherload of...buckeyes! We couldn't find any in Ohio, even at "Buckeye Lake," but here, in southern West Virginia, they covered the ground in abundance. We collected a few to take back with us as souvenirs.

We pulled out of Camp Creek State Park around 11 am and navigated back to I-77 south and drove all day, stopping only a few times for gas and once for some Advil for Joe who felt a migraine coming on.

I don't remember much about Thursday, October 21, 2004, other than savoring the Red Sox's victory from the night before and enjoying the sights as we drove through Virginia, North Carolina, and South Carolina. As we continued south, the clouds lifted, and by the time we crossed into Georgia, it was clear outside. Mid-day, we decided we would try to get to Crooked River State Park on the Atlantic coast, just north of Jacksonville, Florida. Doing so would leave us with only six to seven hours of driving the following day and allow for a daylight homecoming. We anticipated a large dinner with the extended family on our last night together.

A few hours north of our destination, we exited the interstate to fuel up the RV. On our way to a gas station, we passed a roadside stand selling fruit, vegetables, and freshly baked pecan pies. We loaded up on locally grown produce. My father and I loved pecan pie, and we couldn't resist buying one for dessert.

By 5 pm, we were famished but still had two hours of driving left. Joe took responsibility for making dinner on the go. As we barreled south at 70 mph, he cooked burgers on the stove, warmed up some left-over hot dogs and beans, and threw frozen onion rings and chicken wings into the oven. He coordinated the cooking perfectly, and we enjoyed one of our better meals of the trip watching the countryside fly by. The "piece de resistance," as my father later noted, was the locally made pecan pie that the five of us demolished in one sitting.

After eating, Arlan and David cleaned up. An hour or so later, in the dark, we exited I-95 and found our destination. As had happened every night of this trip, we entered the camping area after closing time but still found a great spot to park our RV, under tall southern pine trees that seemed to be growing out of sand dunes. When we stepped outside, there was a moist, salty, ocean breeze. We knew we were closing in on Florida.

I was excited at the prospect of returning home to Rhode Island. I knew I would miss my four traveling companions. I was worried my dad might have a post-trip letdown, though we had already begun encouraging him to plan the next year's follow up adventure. We discussed visiting the Dayton Air Museum, returning to Uhrichsville, touring the Rail Museum in Dennison, trying to figure out some of the other battles Ferrell had fought in, and maybe tracking down some of Ferrell's living relatives and visiting them. We agreed we would arrange for more time off to avoid feeling pressured.

My father did not write much about the last two days of travel in his journal. He did, however, have some summary comments:

Any way one measures it, retracing the steps of Private JKP Ferrell was a success. We learned a lot about this man. The South had captured him twice before he got out of his teens, at Stones River and at Chickamauga. Both encounters were among the bloodiest of the Civil War. Ironically, Chickamauga is a Cherokee Indian word for "river of death." In both battles, JKP appeared to be in the wrong place at the wrong time. We can only imagine the look of panic on the boy-soldier's face as the Rebs surrounded him and other members of his company.

As of this writing, we have no photo of JKP, and while we know the stature of this teen, his face is clouded, and we can only imagine his facial features. He would probably be clean shaven as his beard would appear as peach fuzz. His eyes were sunken because of fear that comes from battle, etched into his look.

As for me, I received an added bonus in that all members of the Fabulous Five felt they had been a part of something special. We sensed a certain provenance, as if JKP was guiding us along.

In the end, I would say that two bits bought us quite a lot. We only regret that other family members did not get the opportunity to share in this adventure.

CHAPTER 12
The Mallet
Closure

The mallet gave my dad renewed vitality near the end of his life. It led five of us on an unforgettable cross-country motorhome trip. It personalized the Civil War for the trip's participants. Now, over forty years after its discovery, the mallet continues to urge me on, to tie up the details and close the loop.

I sometimes feel that JKP and my dad are sitting together, watching and guiding me. I hope that I am telling the story in a way that sits well with them. I am left with so many questions. What was it like growing up in Uhrichsville, Ohio in the 1850s? What pushed JKP to join the army? What was his homecoming like? Did anyone understand what he'd been through? How did his stay in Andersonville affect his general health and mental well-being? Did he become desensitized to death? And how did that mallet end up in a thrift shop in south Florida? My biggest questions, however, were where did JKP make the mallet and for what purpose?

My father concluded that JKP made the mallet for him, but I'm starting to wonder if perhaps he made it for me. Is he trying to impart his wisdom and help me embrace aging and the changes that come with it? Life is all about perseverance, dealing with the ups and downs. The worst day of my life was undoubtedly better than JKP's best day in Andersonville, and he was imprisoned there for over seven months.

As I contemplate the mallet's significance, I picture Ferrell, dressed in his Union blues with an earnest look on his face, bent over with a pocketknife in one hand and a solid piece of pecan in the other. There was a time when young boys whittled and worked with wood, shaping it into useful or at least decorative objects. Today, if most American men were handed a split of wood and a carving tool, very few could fashion anything special. When a man makes a re-markable item with his hands, he has something to carve his initials into for posterity. If the piece represents extraordinary workman-ship, the proud artisan leaves his legacy for others to marvel over as the crafted item passes through their hands.

I am impressed with Ferrell's carving. The small hammer, though rough in detail, is perfectly proportioned and gracefully wrought. It is not ornate, but the simple design is more than ade-quate. I wonder if JKP was proud of the end result and glad to claim it with his initials, his hometown, and the name of the place that so brutally tested him. I am astounded at the life this man lived, the deprivations he suffered and the atrocities he witnessed. The Civil War was the greatest test of the American Experiment. There was no outside enemy, no invading force. The fields fought over were stained only with the blood of Americans. Ferrell's mallet randomly connected the five of us to that time period, to that national tragedy. It heightened our awareness and deepened our reverence for those who sacrificed.

When I hold the mallet in my hands, I wonder where will I carve my initials? I can't make anything worthy out of wood. I quickly remind myself that two amazing children were carefully and lovingly raised in the home Joy and I created. They are extraordinary, balanced and resourceful, and I am proud to be replaced by them. I have had a long career as a pediatric cardiologist. My diligence and meticulous oversight have wrought both healing and some loss as its legacy. But what about my initials? What will I make with my hands?

I gaze down at my hands and notice blisters in various stages of healing. I chuckle to myself. The rock walls! I have slowly built and repaired old-fashioned New England stone walls around my property. I have gotten pretty good at it. The walls carry my "initials." They will remain long after I have departed. They will persevere, mostly because of the herculean effort it would take to remove them. Unfortunately, they are not something I can carve my initials into and not something that a future American can hold in his or her hand. But they will do.

Nine months after completing the motorhome trip, my father died, suddenly and unexpectedly, though he had continued to deteriorate from his underlying neurologic disorder. He was planning the itinerary for motorhome trip number two at the time of his death. Two years later, my brother-in-law Arlan, suffering the ravages of polycythemia vera, joined my father. As I write this, I envision them together, smiling, looking down at my narrative efforts. The mallet still connects me to both of them. I am grateful JKP.

The Ferrell story ends here, and some would argue that perhaps that's enough for one book. However, I never would have chronicled the previous story had I not embarked on a second journey, an interstate bike trip, which superficially might seem completely unrelated, but viscerally, to me, felt very similar. This second journey connected me back to the first and compelled me to bring Ferrell's story to life in written form, almost as a historical prelude. So, I must continue on with my next story, which is also not really mine, but rather my friend Dave's story. As you may recall, my acute, late night acknowledgement of Dave's miraculous survival in Vietnam was the first "sign" that pushed me to begin this writing project.

DBHS Basketball 1974

JZ, Jimmy ("Hook"), and Greg

My Father

High School

Freshman at MSU

Army draftee

MP in Japan

Wedding Day

Modern Day Civil War Odyssey

The "chalet"

Andersonville – staking out the outer stockade and the dead-line

Cemetery at Andersonville

The fabulous five at Stone's River

The Ferrell burial plot

JKP's grave with the mallet

Typical RI rock wall

PART 2

CHAPTER 13
A Crazy Idea

Our neighborhood, Plum Beach, sits on a hill leading down to Narragansett Bay. In 2015, my friend Dave and his wife Stephanie lived one street up and one block over from us. They have since moved up another street. The first homes in our neighborhood, a cluster of summer cottages, were built over 100 years ago for the wealthy citizenry of Providence. The residents moved down from the city during the summer and took advantage of the cooling waters of the bay. Families spent days on the sandy beach and evenings playing softball and tennis. Over time, new families built other homes, and most of the original cottages were winterized. At present, most of our neighbors are year-round inhabitants, though there is still a summertime crowd that lives elsewhere the rest of the year. One by one they trickle back like robins during late spring and early summer.

During the warmer months, Plum Beach is a beehive of activity. Within the confines of the neighborhood, at the bottom of the hill and on the beach, sits the Plum Beach Club with a mooring field out front, a wide sandy beach, a small dock, and a weathered, cedar shingled club building. About 200 yards up the hill from the club sit four clay tennis courts, also for members' use. There is a constant stream of foot traffic, mostly young kids, up and down the hill every day of the summer, and our house sits right in the middle of it.

Dave's former home has a sizable backyard with a few huge maples. In one corner there is a large rock outcropping pointing up through the ground. A few years prior to moving, Dave and Steph cleared brush from around this odd shaped massive piece of rock, and they noted several recesses in the solid granite, big enough to hold pieces of wood and build fires. They created a series of fire pits, on the ground around the front and rear faces of stone, and in the recesses in the rock itself. On cool nights, neighbors often congregated around "Fire Rock." The burning embers and heated rock surface glowed deeply orange and provided ambient warmth. Fire Rock became the end of the evening watering hole, sometimes with ten to twenty neighbors showing up, sitting and talking well past midnight.

In the late spring of 2015, Dave cleared brush from another outcropping of ledge next to fire rock that was filled with thick, tangled roots of brambles and small bushes. He spent several days digging, chopping, and cutting roots until he unearthed a five-foot-wide and three-foot-deep hollowed-out crater in the solid rock. He sealed small cracks and filled the large recess with water, forming a small pond into which he put an oxygenator to create an ambience of moving water. The pool was almost as big as a bathtub. Inspired, Dave then got especially industrious and constructed an arching bridge next to the water pool and a large platform treehouse in an aged maple about twenty feet away. By mid-June, he finished all these projects, and fire rock and the yard's other attractions became even more of a focal point for neighbors. Late at night, as people were winding down from parties at the beach club or elsewhere but not quite ready to turn in, they met at fire rock.

Sometimes, Joy, Steph, Dave, and I would be the last four, casually talking as fires in the rock face smoldered, our feet dangling in the cooling water of the small rock pond. I remember the feel of the misty summer night air, the warmth emanating from fire rock, the quiet of the late hour, the comfort of being with one's closest friends. It was as if time slowed. Occasionally, Dave and I would outlast our wives. During such late-night conversations, I learned bits and pieces about his Vietnam experience.

Dave never advertised the fact that he was a decorated veteran, a former Army Ranger. He didn't let his service or war exploits define him. In fact, initially, I had to get a few drinks into him before broaching the topic. He would make a comment, and I'd gently probe. Over time, I learned his story. At least I thought I did. I later discovered that my understanding of his Vietnam experience was incomplete, missing several key details.

I didn't realize this as the two of us sat in Dave's backyard on a summer evening in late June 2015. I had brought with me a bottle of Alsatian white wine, and Dave and I slowly sipped it, savoring its fruit and dryness. By midnight, we had killed that bottle. As Dave got up and deliberately made his way across the grass and into his house to get us a nightcap, I thought back on our previous decade in Plum Beach.

Joy and I had met Steph and Dave on the tennis court— Thursday evenings, mixed doubles. During our early years in Plum Beach, we had a small group of regulars. One Thursday evening, Dave was out of town on business, and Joy invited Stephanie over for dinner after tennis. Our friendship began that night and then grew.

The four of us started playing tennis three to four days a week. In the winter, we rented court time indoors every Saturday afternoon. Most of the time it was Joy and me against Steph and Dave, but sometimes we mixed it up. I have memories of extended games going long past dusk, often ended by one of my daughters tromping up the hill from our house to remind us it was time for dinner. I was so content then—good friends and the girls still at home. I don't think I ever felt as peaceful with life as I did when my kids were young, going through their formative years. I appreciated every second of existence; life made complete sense.

Thinking back, I can still feel the comfort of daylight fading and see the burning lights in our kitchen as Joy and I walked down the hill from the tennis courts to find Meg working at the dining room table, finishing the last of her homework, and Kate, a long-legged, braces-wearing pre-teen, complaining about our inadequate parenting. Often Steph and Dave grabbed some food and joined us for a late dinner. We would grill outside and watch the day end.

A few years after we met Dave, he began having trouble with his left hand, initially only obvious on the tennis court when he tossed the ball for his powerful serve. Over the next few years, his left arm weakness progressed, and he developed an intention tremor and unsteady gait. The brunt of Parkinson's disease gradually settled in. His consulting business clients often called on Dave to address large crowds. He became self-conscious about his tremor and speech, and he cut back and then closed his business. He started taking pictures, dabbled in a computer software application for charitable fundraising, and then started writing. Despite the Parkinson's, he remained active.

With time, I became increasingly fond of Dave, feeling like he was a brother. He possessed a tenacity, the likes of which I had not witnessed before. He was genuine, and I admired his humility, fairness, and honesty. A radiant joy burned from within, obvious to those who knew him best. His smile, twisted and slow to form, always lifted the mood of those around him. His laughter, deep and booming, came straight from the gut. But it was his eyes that were the window to his emotions. As his Parkinson's disease progressed and increasingly masked his facial expressions, I learned to read him by subtle changes in the lines of his face and the altered glow in his eyes.

Dave suffered a string of health problems preceding and following the summer of 2015—worsening Parkinson's, loss of central vision, prostate cancer, and then lung cancer. Despite the challenges imposed by his multiple illnesses, he did not lose his positive spirit or his competitiveness. It was that fighting spirit along with his leadership qualities and wartime service that earned Dave the designated role of "neighborhood hero." Even the kids of the neighborhood fully respected Dave. It was okay to annoy other adults, but it was an unwritten rule that none of the kids messed with Dave. They all had his back.

I heard the back slider open and then close. I looked up and saw Dave slowly shuffling across his backyard to where I was sitting, the remains of a bottle of sauvignon blanc in his hands. He refilled both our glasses. It was now well past midnight as we sipped the cold sauvignon blanc. The wine was not as sweet and fruity as the Alsatian white, though still very dry. It had a strong mineral aftertaste, a little ending kick. We moved over to the rock pond and sat on its edge with our feet in the water. It was silent around us except for the sound of water gurgling.

As I sat and relaxed, I felt very content in the tranquil setting. I pictured a younger Dave next to me—a badass Army Ranger. I looked over at him and asked, "You ever been to the Vietnam War Memorial in Washington?"

From some of our previous conversations, I knew that the North Vietnamese had shot down Dave's helicopter. He had just turned nineteen years old. Five Ranger teammates died instantly; Dave walked away. I also knew that Dave's story was well known within the Vietnam Army Ranger community, but not really by anyone else. I suspected the event had deeply affected him, though he compartmentalized things so well that only those closest to him might sense that deep within there was a suppressed seriousness or darkness. Survivor's guilt? Post-traumatic stress? Pent up anger? Fear? Demons? I imagined a little of all.

After a few glasses of wine, the usual barriers to honest conversation often grow thinner. I wondered if Dave had visited the Wall, had he searched for and found his Ranger teammates' names on it. He looked at me with a distant, sad look in his eyes. After a few moments he replied, "I've seen the Vietnam Wall in D.C. It wasn't easy for me, and I don't think I would go back without a lot of support. I'm not sure why I'm sitting here talking to you, and other guys' names are on the Wall."

I probed further. "So, you haven't come to terms with your war experience? Your survival?"

Dave shook his head. "No, I suppose not. At least not completely."

I felt badly, like I had exposed Dave, opened festering wounds only partly healed by time.

As I sat there looking at Dave, I reminded myself of his amazing inner strength and appreciation of life. Maybe it was the wine, but as I contemplated the pain he carried inside and the burdens from his past war experience, my mind started spinning. Parkinson's had affected Dave's mobility, but from the few bike rides we had taken over the years, I knew that he was still a strong cyclist. When pedaling, he rode straight and true. I knew this was not unique to Dave. One of the weird things about individuals with Parkinson's is that they can often ride a bike with relative ease, long after they've lost the ability to run, and even walk, without assistance.

Suddenly, I blurted out, "Dave, I think we should ride our bikes from Plum Beach to the Wall in Washington. We should ride for your teammates. We should find their names and honor their memories. You, me, and anyone else crazy enough to join us."

I knew I had struck a nerve. Dave looked up at me. His eyes twinkled as a big smile slowly formed on his face. "When do you want to do this?" he asked.

I replied, "Next fall, mid-September—over a year away. It will give us time to think things through and prepare accordingly."

He continued smiling and responded, "I'm in."

Over the next few months, Dave and I occasionally revisited our pact to ride our bikes to the Wall. After a glass of wine, we'd smile at each other and joke about it, though inside, both of us were dead serious.

The summer of 2015 gradually wound down. In late August, my younger daughter Kate began her senior year of high school, and in mid-September, my other daughter Meg left for a year to teach in Thailand. I had experienced an overwhelming sadness when Meg had left for college four years earlier, and I was worried that it would be even harder the following September when Kate, my "little buddy," moved away. Joy and I looked forward to her senior year of high school, excited to watch her compete in tennis and basketball, but part of me dreaded her eventual graduation and departure.

When I proposed September 2016 as the target date for riding to D.C., it was partly based on selfishness and self-preservation. I thought the challenge of biking all day would be the perfect distraction to the perceived major life change I feared. Dave was well aware of this. He had been one of my pillars of support following Meg's departure; he knew how my mind worked. I thought that no matter how emotionally depleted I might be, riding a bike all day in the great outdoors would be rejuvenating. I envisioned supporting Dave on what I considered a heroic trek (on his part) as mutually advantageous—a perfect adventure.

At the time, looking ahead, I often wondered how Dave envisioned the trip. Did he have reservations? Did he see it as a journey of discovery and redemption? Did he feel like he was spitting into the face of Parkinson's? YOU WILL NOT SLOW ME DOWN!

In truth, at that time I knew very little about Dave's early life or his service in Vietnam. He had been born in Alaska, one of thirteen children. When Dave was eight, his father and an older brother drowned while fishing. His widowed mother moved her large family to North Dakota, remarried, and had two more children. When Dave turned eighteen, he joined the Army and volunteered for Airborne training. Shortly thereafter, he received orders for Vietnam, unsure of why and where he was going. He was a teenager, naive to the ways of the world. I assumed he grew up quickly.

Once in Vietnam, Dave volunteered for Ranger training. I knew that Vietnam Ranger units were inserted behind enemy lines to do reconnaissance patrols. On September 20, 1970, the fateful morning of his last day of active combat duty, I pictured Dave's helicopter hovering at tree top level, suddenly hit by enemy fire, with Dave and his teammates thrown to the ground. I envisioned Dave landing in a water-filled ditch and lying there, unconscious, until he was eventually found and rescued. For years, that was the image I held in my mind. It seemed plausible that one could survive such an event.

Dave had strong feelings for his teammates who died that day. Every one of those young men had a story, a family, friends. When you read about casualties of war, it objectively seems to boil down to numbers. But how many of the ripples from each death turn into tsunamis that bring down spouses, parents, siblings, and friends? So many people affected way beyond the casualty count.

I knew that Dave had a deep appreciation for this. I suspected that for his own self-preservation, he forced himself to move on. For decades he didn't outwardly question things. He made no attempts to reconnect with those still alive—those directly or indirectly affected by the events of that morning. He returned from Vietnam, resumed his education, earned a master's degree, enjoyed a successful professional career, married, had an amazing son, and lived his life fully. I believe he thought that anything less would be

144

disrespectful to the memory of his fallen teammates. When asked a direct question about Vietnam, Dave always politely gave a succinct answer. He did not expand. He did not let Vietnam define him.

2015 rolled into 2016. In early 2016, Dave and I started telling others about our plan to ride bikes from Plum Beach to the Vietnam Wall the coming fall. Our wives and friends were mostly amused. During several previous late-night sessions around fire rock, Dave and I had proposed other ambitious undertakings, some of which had come to fruition; many that had not. I think initially, most thought that this crazy scheme would also die a natural death. No one took us too seriously.

In the late spring of 2016, I sent an e-mail to neighbors hoping others would join us on our journey. At this point, Dave and I did not own working bikes, and neither of us had ridden one for over a year. A few friends were serious cyclists and half-heartedly expressed an interest in coming along. In the end, they were unable to commit. By late May 2016, Dave and I had garnered enthusiastic support for our quest, but we had been unable to recruit additional riders. And then I thought of Coleman.

Coleman was a former neighbor who had abruptly picked up and moved his family to Florida six years previously. He and his wife Linda were part of our closest circle of friends at the time of their departure. Coleman was a "no bullshit," self-made man who could do anything and wasn't afraid to tell anyone what was on his mind. He made his living as a private detective, but he was an outstanding carpenter and mechanical genius. He could take a boat or engine apart, fix it, and put it back together again. In some ways—not the least of which included his abrupt departure to Florida—he reminded me of my father, and even more of my brother Joe. He also had that crazy edge to him. I foresaw this particular challenge as one he'd be unable to pass up. I pictured his response, "Jimmy, that is the dumbest f'ing idea you've ever had. I am most definitely in."

I sent him an e-mail, and he called me the next day, responding exactly as I had anticipated. He, also, did not own a bike.

In mid-June, unbeknownst to Dave, I sent an e-mail to our closest friends explaining what Dave, Coleman, and I were planning to do. I asked if any of them would consider meeting us at the Wall as we rode our bikes into D.C. and then spending the night celebrating in Washington. I was hoping to rent a venue and host an official event honoring Dave and his fallen teammates.

Within 24 hours, I had commitments from over thirty neighbors. I wasn't surprised. Plum Beachers loved supporting worthy causes, and this one was personal. No one wanted to miss a unique opportunity to surprise and honor Dave. The hardest part would be keeping such a big secret—the fact that our entire neighborhood would be converging on Washington, D.C.—from Dave.

CHAPTER 14
No Turning Back

On a Saturday morning in early June 2016, Dave and I drove to the local bike store. After reviewing different models, we selected sleek touring bikes. We also bought forward and rear lights, speedometers, helmets, water bottle holders, and a basic repair kit for each bike.

The next day, Joy took me back to the store to pick up my new, decked out bike. After receiving a quick lecture about my particular model and some of the equipment, I guided my bike out of the store, jumped on, and started cycling north on Route 1-A toward home. As I gained speed, my spirits soared. Feeling the wind in my face was exhilarating, and I experienced no apprehension about the prospect of riding sixty to seventy miles daily for six days. Perhaps I was naïve, but I was not at all intimidated.

From late June through August, Dave and I did weekly group rides, usually twenty to thirty miles. Sometimes it was just the two of us, and at other times, Stephanie and others joined. One time we had eight riders, including my nephew David who was visiting from Florida, and Coleman, who was in town on business. Coleman had restored an old hybrid mountain bike of Dave's to use for the upcoming trip.

Generally, the training rides were great fun, though our friends frequently reminded us that twenty to thirty-mile social group rides once a week were not equivalent to sixty to seventy miles of riding every day for six days straight. I recall conversations with various individuals trying to gently convince me that perhaps I had set my sights too high; that maybe I should reconsider this crazy plan. I especially remember one of my neighbors, David, coming over one evening and sitting with me on our front porch. I sensed concern on his face as he walked up our porch stairs and sat down in the rocker next to me. As we gazed out over my lawn, taking in the beauty of summer's colors with the gleaming blue water of Narragansett Bay in the distance, he was unusually silent, carefully trying to choose his words.

I looked over at him, "Something on your mind David?"

He responded, "I heard Dave wiped out today on your group ride."

I thought back to the morning's ride. We were pedaling on a busy road paralleling Narragansett Beach when a member of our group inadvertently cut in front of Dave and nudged his front tire. Dave lost control, veered wildly off the road, and flew off his bike. He slid across dense grass into a flower bed, his upper body partly hidden behind some low hedges. As Dave's momentum ceased, his head came to rest just in front of a stone wall.

I jumped off my bike and ran over to Dave who was positioned prone on the ground, his head invisible behind a low bush. I saw the stone wall and feared that he had rammed his head into it. Before I reached him, he sat up and looked back at the group of riders, all frozen in place, terrified that he had badly hurt himself.

He smiled, and we all let out a collective sigh of relief. I pulled Dave up. His arms and legs were bruised and he had a few deep scrapes but no major injuries. He hobbled over to his bike, righted it, and climbed on as if nothing had happened. He continued onward and the rest of us followed.

I was appreciative of David's concern. I explained, "Yes, it was a freak accident. Dave is fine."

With an insistent tone, David replied, "You know, sixty miles of riding in one day is a very long bike ride. Sixty miles of riding in one day for six straight days is completely off the charts…insane…nonsense, especially for a group of misguided individuals WHO ARE NOT EVEN BIKE RIDERS! I have been your neighbor for the past eighteen years, and I HAVE NEVER SEEN YOU ON A BIKE!"

I smiled back, "David, trust me. It will be a piece of cake. And when we successfully complete this ride, I will remind you of this conversation."

He sat quietly for another five minutes, clearly annoyed with me, certain that this mad escapade of ours was doomed to fail.

Sensing his irritation, I continued, "David, I promise you I will get Dave to the Wall and back to Plum Beach without a scratch on his body. If you can talk Dave out of the ride, I will surrender to your concerns, but you aren't going to talk me out of it."

David stood up, looked down at me and said, "I thought you were supposed to be a smart doctor."

I smiled at him. "Well I am a doctor, but I would never tell anyone I was a rational human being. Have a little faith!"

With a huff, he turned, carefully climbed down the stairs to the driveway, and then looked back and retorted, "Oh, the ignorance of youth…"

"David, I'm almost sixty years old. You can't blame this one on youth."

I laughed to myself as I watched him walk out to the road, down the hill, around a corner, and gradually out of sight.

On the last Saturday of August 2016, Joy and I moved Kate into her freshman dorm at the University of Vermont. We stayed in Burlington overnight and departed early the next morning. I thought I would be an emotional wreck, trapped in a vice of despondency, but I was all right. I was sad and felt a bit empty, but not overwhelmingly so.

When we returned home, I jumped onto my bike and went for a long ride. I remember taking in my surroundings and thinking, "Life goes on." The leaves were still fluttering in the breeze, the sun was still shining, and people were out, walking their dogs and enjoying the beautiful day. Nothing was visibly different except for the small fact that my little girl had grown up and was now embarking on a journey of self-discovery and growth. In my heart, I was very proud of and happy for her. In my gut, I wanted to race back to Burlington and bring her home.

As I pedaled that last Sunday of August, I knew that in one week, Dave, Coleman, probably Stephanie (though she had not yet fully committed), and I would leave from Plum Beach and ride into the "great wide open." We had a rough idea of the route we would take, and we had reserved hotel rooms for the first two nights. We figured once we were past Labor Day weekend, it would be easy to secure lodging. I went to bed that night missing Kate, feeling a little edgy about the upcoming trip, and thinking I needed to buckle down and survive the work week.

It is interesting that Dave and I never had a frank conversation about how either of us viewed the upcoming journey. It was as if we had blindly made a pact to ride, so we were bound to do it— end of story: dudes being dudes, not really thinking things through or deeply considering the implications or the possibility of failure. Same with Coleman. The three of us never expressed any reservations, at least not to one another.

I realize in retrospect that my perspective was completely one dimensional. The journey would be immensely easier for me than it would be for Dave. I was facing some minor life changes. He was dealing with multiple major medical problems. He was the one personally connected to Vietnam and the soldiers we planned to honor. He was the one who risked opening old wounds and confronting old demons as he grappled to make peace with his Vietnam War experience.

I asked Dave to share his memory of the months leading up to our departure. He wrote the following:

Jim invited me to contribute to this chapter, as I am now one of the subjects of his writing. I agreed to be the "set up" man. Here is the gist of it. On September 20, 1970, I was with a six-man Ranger team in Vietnam riding on a Huey helicopter preparing for an insertion into the DMZ. Just north of Firebase Alpha 4, the chopper took enemy fire, crashed, and burst into flames. I walked away from the crash that morning, the only survivor of my team. I have done battle with my Vietnam experience every day since then.

I was not in such a good place in 2016 as conversations about riding bicycles from our Rhode Island homes to the Vietnam War Memorial in Washington became more serious. In fact, I was a physical, emotional, and mental "train-wreck." They say God never gives you more than you can handle. Still, it seemed as if I'd received more than my fair share of tragedy and bad luck. The VA docs diagnosed me with lung cancer earlier that spring, and I was in a sorry state.

At the time of that diagnosis, I viewed my lot in life as made up more of burdens than blessings. I was still recovering from prostate cancer for which I had received a total of 45 localized radiation treatments in 2015. I had awakened one morning in May 2015 unable to see clearly. I had lost my central vision. I was already eleven years into the diagnosis of Parkinson's disease. I was also dealing with residual emotional issues originating from my war experience. Now, lung cancer.

Most of the time, I didn't talk about it. I felt others might see a plea for help as a sign of weakness. And weakness was not a characteristic familiar to me. Some friends and acquaintances refer to my actions as heroic. This kind of praise makes me uncomfortable when I survived by simply being in the right place at the right time. Or they think my contemporary struggle to deal with war's residual damage is heroic. I know that the speaker intends nothing but to honor me, or people like me. The trouble is, free use of the term lessens the meaning of it to those who were real heroes. And I can name quite a few of those with whom I served.

My friends and neighbors have elevated me to such a lofty place that I am bound to fail them. They treat me not as a survivor but as a hero. It is as if I am a proxy for that place in American history that most have only read of or heard about through older siblings. One friend's brother served. Another was a half-hearted protester. Yet another had school deferments. But many were too young (or in the case of my wife Stephanie, not yet born) to have had any idea what the war was about. I concluded I could educate them about the war and keep the names of my fallen teammates alive.

When it comes to the helicopter crash, I have blamed God, the universe, weather, my commanding officers, bad luck, the North Vietnamese, the pilot. Tragedy demands (and often defies) examination and explanation. Why and how did this happen? We try to understand, to make sense of it. Why did I walk away relatively unscathed from a crash most observers described as "unsurvivable?" Was my survival a matter of serendipity? Fate? For what purpose was my life spared? Anyone in my position would ask the questions.

I have subscribed to each of the usual explanations at one time or another, depending on my state of mind at the time. Mostly, I tried not to dwell on the fact that so far, I had cheated death and side-stepped meaningful infirmity. I have tried to live my life in such a way to honor my teammates who had fallen. I feel that I must do everything better, or if not better, then at least with meaningful effort. I have not sought this position of being a "poster boy" for Vietnam. Others have thrust it upon me.

What we are talking about here, though, was my level of fitness to undertake a 400-mile bicycle ride and my readiness to open doors to my Vietnam war experience that I had kept locked for a long time. I said "yes" to Jim's suggestion that we ride without considering the implications. True, I have an athletic past. I had run marathons and ridden my bike over the Rockies. I was captain of my high school basketball and football teams. And I had humped 100-pound rucksacks up and down the mountains of Vietnam. So, I had confidence in what I USED to be able to expect out of my body thirty or forty years ago. The fitness of my mind, not so much.

Then and now, Parkinson's and loss of my vision are what give me the most problems. I still played tennis in 2016, though poorly. I hadn't been on a bicycle for years. I golfed some days very well. Until this past year, I often won long drive contests. But I was thirty pounds overweight, with Parkinson's and bad vision. I sometimes freeze when I start walking. I might stumble although I rarely fall. The bradykinesia results in my taking twice as long to do even the simplest things, like putting on my socks or tying my shoelaces. I drool a lot, and my speech is horrible.

Shortly after I agreed to the bike ride, my V.A. doctors diagnosed my cancer after picking up a "spot" on my lung during a routine chest x-ray. At the time, I thought a diagnosis of lung cancer was a death sentence. My doctors classified my cancer as stage II adenocarcinoma. Not the worst kind of cancer if caught early on.

Initially, my doctors gave me a few weeks to see if the spot would resolve. Then I traveled to the Boston V.A. hospital for a P.E.T. scan. Again, a negative report. My surgeon proposed going in and taking a biopsy of the tumor. If he found the tumor cancerous, he would cut it out, without delay. In March 2016, I had a left upper lobectomy. The surgeon entered my chest through a small incision under my left armpit. He gave me a positive post-surgery report. He felt he had excised it all. There were no signs of cancer in the lymph nodes, and all margins were clear.

I had now survived two cancers, and Parkinson's had forced me into a medical retirement by the time I turned 61 years old. The V.A. had declared me 100% combat-disabled. Over the past decade, the Veteran's Administration has approved disability claims made by Vietnam combat veterans for prostate cancer, lung cancer, and Parkinson's disease (along with other conditions), as presumptively caused by Agent Orange. I am not aware that I had direct exposure to the chemical; in other words, I never handled it. But we did slog through Agent Orange defoliated jungle. The DMZ, where we operated, was a wasteland of barren foliage and huge bomb craters filled with water. On the day of the crash, my rescuers found me crawling out of a large bomb crater, the water, no doubt, contaminated by Agent Orange.

So that is a more detailed back-story, miserable sounding I suspect. However, I felt pretty good as the summer of 2016 approached. I had just received positive preliminary reports from my surgeon. I had a good three months to prepare for the ride which we had decided would start Labor Day weekend, arriving in D.C. on September 10, 2016.

In June I bought a new touring bike. I went into the summer thinking I was as ready as I could be. I was uncertain and a bit anxious about my abilities, but I think nervously excited about the journey we were about to attempt. God knows, it was time for some reconciliation in my life.

CHAPTER 15
Another Trip of a Lifetime

Within our group of close friends in Plum Beach, there is one guy who I refer to as "the big idea guy." His name is Andy Kinnecom. Andy has navigated some major life challenges. He watched his first wife suffer and then die from widespread intra-abdominal cancer. From the depth of his pain, he ultimately emerged stronger and more cognizant of life's blessings. With time, aided by the love and support of two amazing daughters, he reclaimed his positive spirit. He embraced life—the good and the bad. Andy also possessed a deep-seated love and admiration for Dave. During Dave's many health challenges, Andy often rearranged his work schedule to make sure Dave made it to medical appointments.

Andy's mindset is the ultimate "go big or go home." No idea is too outlandish. When I told him about the bike trip, he was one of the few who didn't laugh. Instead, his response was, "Awesome! I wish I could go with you." At the time, Andy did not ride, and he was too busy with his several businesses and building projects to join us. However, when I invited our neighbors to meet us in D.C. to welcome Dave at the Wall, he and his wife Margaret were the first to commit.

Andy volunteered to learn as much as he could about Dave's fateful morning in Vietnam—the individuals involved and the teammates who died that day—if and/or when Dave volunteered information. Andy and I both knew we had an incomplete picture of what really happened the morning of September 20, 1970. We were not sure how much Dave remembered. We suspected we might learn more as Dave became comfortable traveling into the past on the upcoming bike ride. Any information I gleaned from Dave I would communicate to Andy. He would then do focused research and report details back to me so that I could enlighten the others. Andy would serve as our Plum Beach connection, our cord to home base. He also agreed to coordinate the group surprising Dave at the wall and to serve as emcee at our party in Washington on the night of our arrival. Andy and I planned to stay in close contact throughout the ride.

The weekend before we left, the tentative plan, as Dave knew it, was for him, Coleman, probably Steph, and me to ride with all our gear and for Joy to drive down and meet us in D.C. six days later. If Stephanie decided not to ride with us, she would travel with Joy. Dave had no awareness that there would be a much larger welcoming assemblage at the Wall.

Amazingly, we had kept this a secret from him all summer, though barely. There had been a few close calls, like the time our friend Ed came up to Steph and Dave at a beach club party a month before our departure and said, "Lisa and I were thinking about going down a few days early and enjoying the sights."

When Ed realized what he had said and who he was talking to, he immediately stopped talking, as if frozen. He stood there, mouth agape, and stared uneasily at Dave and Steph.

Dave looked at Ed, then Steph, and then back at Ed and said, "Where are you going?"

Ed stammered, "I don't really know." He then abruptly turned and wandered off.

Stephanie looked over at Dave who appeared confused and said, "That was unusual." She then walked over to a group of friends, laughing as soon as her back was turned on Dave, wondering if Ed's weird exchange had raised any suspicion.

Or another time when Steph, Dave, and I took a break in the middle of one of our rides. We had cycled to Point Judith Lighthouse, about fifteen miles south of Plum Beach. We rode onto the grassy oceanfront area leading to the lighthouse and got off our bikes. Dave and I sat on adjacent benches and looked out at the deep blue, rolling waves of the Atlantic Ocean merging with the calmer, gray water at the mouth of the Narragansett Bay. It was a clear summer day, and hundreds of sailboats dotted the water in front of us. As we drank from our water bottles, Stephanie, who still hadn't committed to the ride, walked over and said, "I'm considering flying home from Washington with the Burditts." Tim and Lisa Burditt were two of our good friends.

Dave set his water bottle on the bench and looked over at Stephanie with a confused look on his face. Realizing what she'd said, Stephanie tried to cover. She glared back at Dave, silent.

With an incredulous tone, Dave said, "You're flying back from Washington with the Burditts?"

Steph curtly replied, "I didn't say that." She then turned and briskly walked back to her bike. Looking back over her shoulder, she impatiently yelled, "Let's get going."

I avoided eye contact with Dave and pretended I didn't hear any of the conversation. As I slowly strolled over to my bike, I chuckled to myself. Dave walked behind me. We mounted our bikes and rode back to Plum Beach, no further comments made about flying or the Burditts. After I waved good-bye to Steph and Dave, I continued down the hill to my house wondering if our cover had been blown. It turns out it had not. The fact that spouses don't listen that intently to one another or take too seriously what they do hear worked in our favor.

Mid-week preceding our Sunday departure, there was a massive hurricane, Hermine, heading up the East Coast of the United States. Initial projections had it traveling directly over the route we planned to follow. As the weekend approached, things looked increasingly ominous, with Hermine threatening the New Jersey coastline. Friday afternoon, Stephanie expressed anxiety about Dave riding off with Coleman and me into the face of a major hurricane. She was still undecided about joining us. Dave and I tried to convince her to come along; we discussed taking a support car and trading off driving. I suspect the threatening weather and her protective instinct for Dave solidified Stephanie's decision to join the biking team.

Stephanie had done several group rides with Dave and me over the course of the summer, and she was a stronger cyclist than both of us. She owned an old but solid road bike, and she had already taken the week off from work. The thought of having a car, just in case, was appealing to all of us. As we continued watching the weather forecasts, Hermine had us worried that we might need to delay our departure or possibly even abort our planned journey.

Not known to me heading into the ride, Dave had set up a Facebook page, "Ranger Team 1-8 Tour." At the time, I was new to Facebook, but Dave, Steph, and Coleman felt it would be the best way to share our exploits with supporters and friends. Dave asked me if I would post daily updates, and I obliged, taking on the unofficial role of trip "journalist," though all four of us contributed posts as the ride progressed. The following two posts preceded our departure.

Facebook Post (Dave) Friday, September 2, 2016.

Well, the time is upon us. There is no backing out. On Sunday, I will be joined by my wife Steph and my good friends Jimmy Z and Cole in setting forth on a 400+ mile bike ride from my home in Rhode Island to the Vietnam Memorial Wall in D.C. We may be facing down the rain and wind of Hermine, though we hope the hurricane blows off course from the mid-Atlantic.

Facebook Post (Dave) Saturday, September 3, 2016

It is 10:30 pm. I am a few hours away from "The Ride," wondering why I feel so nervous. Okay, I've run two marathons, and biked across the Rockies, and have a general history of toughness. But in three days, I turn 65, and I suddenly don't feel so tough anymore. The "I am invincible" façade collapsed around me through a series of illnesses over the past ten years. I previously took pride in thinking, "You can kick the shit out of me, but you'll never get me to say, Uncle." Now I just feel humbled. Grateful beyond measure that I have my wife Stephanie and that she is riding with me, and that my good friends Jim Z and Cole are our companions.

I am making this ride to honor my teammates lost too young some 46 years ago. I have regretted without measure my inability over the years to properly recognize their ultimate sacrifice and acknowledge the deep sense of loss felt by their families. I have failed in my duty, and I hope that through this ride I can make amends as the one who lived. As my friends and acquaintances, I invite you along on this journey of remembrance. This is about me, that is true, and I can't avoid that fact. But I hope that by the time we pull up to the Wall, you will have learned more about these brave men with whom I had the honor of serving. I WILL make the Wall.

One of Dave's high school friends, Mike Killoran, responded to Dave's post with the following:

Yesterday, we were Man-Boys, some were spared, and some got dumped on. Only those left behind still deal with the pain. We're

James W. Ziegler, M.D.

proud of what you have done and what you have become. This is not about You but the part of You that is Them. What a great way to let it out. We will be following you. Good luck and be safe.

CHAPTER 16
The Road Beckons:
Riding for Harold

Day 1 (Sunday. September 4, 2016)

The night before the ride, the four of us slept fitfully—probably a combination of excitement mixed with a bit of apprehension. While we tossed and turned, Hurricane Hermine veered eastward and headed out to sea. We expected to wake up to gale force winds blowing in from the south with high humidity. Instead, intensely blue skies, dry, calm air, and temperature in the mid-sixties—superb riding conditions. I interpreted the altered and merciful path of Hermine as a promising omen for our trip.

At approximately 6:30 am, Steph, Dave, and Coleman showed up at our house with their bikes. Given the change in weather, we debated the need for a support car. We had already decided that Stephanie was joining us, and after a short discussion, we unanimously agreed that a car would add a measure of safety and comfort. It would certainly make time on our bikes more enjoyable.

In addition, Coleman and I were a bit worried about Dave's stability on his bike with heavy saddle bags hanging off the rear. We had witnessed him wipe out the day before during a practice run loaded down with gear. He had veered uncontrollably off the road, thankfully, onto my front yard, which cushioned his fall.

Joy volunteered her Subaru Outback, and Stephanie, Coleman, and I agreed to trade off driving every ten miles with Dave grabbing a shift any time he needed a break. Dave would ride his bike whenever and as much as he wanted.

The four of us were determined to start the ride together, on bikes. This meant we needed someone to drive the car for the first leg of our trip. Thrilled to help out, Joy and our friend Judyann devised a plan to meet us at a drop point in southern Rhode Island.

There was an air of anticipation and excitement as we congregated in our kitchen. Joy had concocted a crockpot breakfast creation that slow-cooked overnight, and by morning, our house smelled like an old-fashioned breakfast diner. As we sat around our kitchen table, we discussed some of the logistics of the ride. To honor Dave's Ranger teammates, we decided to devote each day of the ride to one of the five men. That day, our first day, we would honor Dave's team leader, Harold Sides.

As we finished breakfast, one of our good friends, Mike Denci, stopped by to lead us in a departure prayer. The four riders, Joy, and Mike stood in a circle in our kitchen holding hands as Mike prayed for our safety, health, and happiness on the adventure we were about to undertake. The six of us then sat back down at the table, and I asked Dave to tell us about Harold.

At first, Dave seemed uncomfortable. He had a pained look in his eyes. It was clear he had to reach within and extract memories long hidden and/or suppressed. As I watched him, I felt conflicted, worried that perhaps I had underestimated the emotional toll this trip might take on him. There we were, pre-departure, and already I fretted we might be overwhelming him. Maybe this trip was not such a good idea.

We sat quietly for a few moments, the other five of us patiently and respectfully waiting. Then Dave looked up and smiled. It was as if he had suddenly decided it was time to move forward and in doing so, reconnect with his past. Without pause, he started speaking and told us Harold's story.

Harold was from Dallas, Texas. He was twenty years old the morning of the crash, wise beyond his years as he neared the end of his deployment. He was an experienced soldier, always careful in the bush, fully aware of his duty to keep his men safe. He had a wife and child back home, and he was determined to get back to them. I knew that of all his teammates, Dave especially loved and admired Harold. It saddened us to hear that this exceptional young man left behind a wife and child. I sat there deep in thought, contemplating Harold's life and the influence he had had on Dave.

Other neighbors popped in and out, and then Art, another friend who planned to accompany us on the first leg of our trip, showed up with his bike. The five of us said goodbye to Joy and Mike, climbed onto our bikes, and started up Plum Beach Road. Dave seemed back to his positive, fun-loving self.

Several of our neighbors awoke early to cheer for us as we pedaled up the hill. Some held signs. It reminded me of the beginning of a road race, with an enthusiastic supportive crowd yelling words of encouragement after the starting gun. My adrenaline level was high.

When we reached the top of the hill leading out of our neighborhood, we met up with another neighbor, Janie. At the last minute, she had decided to join our send-off. Her two young daughters jumped up and down, holding signs and yelling after us as she fell in line, and we officially began the ride. Coleman and Stephanie grabbed the lead, initially riding next to one another as they debated best possible starting routes.

I remember the inner peace I experienced that morning as we began riding, the calm and focus. It felt great to be unencumbered in the open air. I was acutely aware of the beauty around me—the greenery and the perfectly blue sky. I was excited and honored to be part of the mission at hand. Everything seemed to be as it should be—positive, doable, and fun. I rode effortlessly with complete confidence that we would get Dave to the Wall.

After ten miles or so, Janie wished us well and turned back. Art continued onward. The clear air and contrasting colors seemed especially dazzling, and we stopped often to take pictures. We stayed on infrequently traveled back country roads and wound our way through rural southern Rhode Island, occasionally losing our way and backtracking.

I experienced one mishap fifteen miles into the trip. We'd stopped to wait for an opportunity to safely cross a busy two-lane road. With the first break in traffic, I jumped onto my bike and pushed forward. I struggled to get my feet into the pedal cages I had attached that morning. I was looking down, not paying attention to what was directly in front of me. I looked up just before hitting the opposite curb head on. I momentarily panicked but quickly relinquished control, fully aware that I was powerless to avoid what was to come. I slammed into the curb, came to an abrupt halt, and catapulted over the handlebars, thankfully landing on soft ground. As I flew through the air, I felt like I was floating in slow motion, and I glanced back to see Coleman exclaiming, "Whaaaaaat the f*********?"

I used my arms to soften my landing and rolled a few times. I was a bit embarrassed but unhurt. My chain had popped off, but no damage to my bike either. Once the others were sure I was okay, they laughed hysterically. Dave, no stranger to wipe outs, joined in. Between chuckles, he yelled out, "Jimmy's no longer a virgin." Sprawled out on the ground, I laughed along with the others, picturing Coleman's confused and somewhat incredulous face as he had watched me sail through the air moments earlier. Lesson learned: ALWAYS keep your eyes on what's in front of you!

As we continued further south, there were fewer homes and long stretches of quiet roads through thick pine forests. The hills grew longer and steeper. My quads burned as I downshifted, often into first gear. After confronting several rolling inclines, my confidence temporarily wavered. Was I really ready to tackle 400-plus miles over unknown terrain?

I contemplated the haphazard way this trip had come together—a random plan hatched by two good friends after a few glasses of wine over a year ago with immediate buy-in from Coleman. The three of us had no idea what stood between Plum Beach and the Vietnam Wall. In essence, we had no clue what we were getting ourselves into. Still, I knew why Dave and I were there. I presumed Coleman was along for the fun and adventure, and also because he passionately loved America and felt indebted to soldiers from all eras.

I glanced up and saw Stephanie in front of me, leaning over her handlebars as she labored up the present incline. Steph's involvement didn't surprise me either. She was brave and adventurous, always up for a challenge. She didn't mind hanging with the guys, and I knew she hoped the ride would bring Dave some closure. She knew Coleman and I were a bit crazy, and I suspect she had a nagging concern that we might race off and leave Dave in the dust to fend for himself. We should have reassured her that this ride was for Dave. He was our focus, and we would not lose sight of that.

On one especially challenging hill, I glanced back and noticed Dave struggling, his bike wobbling a bit. I slowed to let him pass, shouting words of encouragement as he overtook me. Sweat dripped off our faces, stinging our eyes and occasionally blinding us. Despite the difficulty focusing, I saw a determined look on Dave's face. I knew he was not going to be denied. His pace increased, and I stayed behind him, intermittently urging him on, all the while picturing my old teammate Jimmy Morgan, in my face, staring intently at me, "Z, you ready?" I was not going to let Jimmy, or Dave, or Dave's Ranger team leader Harold down. Keep pumping—push down; pull up. I continued pedaling, rejuvenated with my sense of purpose restored. I subconsciously thanked Jimmy for being there, in my head, always pushing me forward when I doubted my resolve. I made a mental note that I needed to reconnect with him and thank him for his impact on my life. I again marveled at Dave's resilience.

After navigating the winding, hilly roads of southern Rhode Island, we met up with Joy and Judyann. We were only ten to fifteen miles from the New London Ferry that would be transporting us across Long Island Sound to Orient Point on the North Fork of Long Island. Because there were no biking routes from our present location across the Thames River into New London, we decided to load our bikes onto the Subaru and drive to the ferry dock *(disclaimer: though we did bike more than 90% of the way from Plum Beach to Washington D.C. on our bikes, there were some parts of the trek that were impossible to cycle in a strategic and/or safe fashion. We were forced to use the car for a few key segments)*. Art threw his bike onto Judyann's car, and the four of us said good-by to Joy, Art, and Judyann.

It was now just the four of us, the committed—or maybe crazy—riders. We drove Joy's Subaru to the ferry dock in silence. It was late morning, and we had covered over thirty miles by bike. We had successfully finished one of the more challenging segments of the ride.

As I drove, I reflected on how different traveling by bike is. In a car, one is confined, only briefly aware of singular passing sites. On a bike, the rider connects with nature, the air, and the ongoing landscape and surroundings that constantly change and hit the senses from every angle. I couldn't wait to get back out there.

We drove the car onto the ferry and then climbed to the upper deck. The sky and water were both deep blue and the air warm and dry. We bought a round of lagers and sat outside enjoying the cool salty breeze. I opened multiple texts from friends back home, mostly chiding me, wondering if I had turned back yet on my crazy quest. There were still some "non-believers" in my expanded group of friends. When I responded no, that I was determined to complete this mission and get Dave safely to the Wall, the texts became universally supportive.

The road out of Orient Point was perfect for cycling with a wide shoulder designated as a bike route. We pedaled past scenic farms and vineyards and through quiet neighborhoods and quaint little towns. Around 6 pm, we pulled into the Comfort Inn in Medford, New York, just less than halfway down Long Island. Dave had driven the last leg, and he met us at the hotel. I had only driven once and felt very fortunate. It had been such a perfect day for riding.

We checked into the hotel and carried our bikes up to our rooms, Steph and Dave in one and Coleman and I in another. After we washed the road grime from our faces, we met downstairs in the communal area. Dave and I posted on Facebook while Stephanie updated friends and Coleman did laundry.

Facebook Post (Dave) Sunday, September 4, 2016

The day is done. 75 biking miles. It was a hard day. I can't pretend otherwise. And I am the slowest rider of the four of us. I do all right on straightaways, but my legs don't seem to have the strength they used to. But my riding mates are patient and cheer me on, so all is good.

We rode for Harold Sides today. Harold was my team leader. He did his best to keep us free from harm, rarely seeking to engage the enemy, but he made us a formidable force when we did.

Later, lying in bed, I thought back on the day's events. At around 2 pm, we had turned off the designated route onto a tree-lined drive and followed signs to a seafood restaurant. The restaurant sat back from the road on a hill that gently sloped down to the water. We seated ourselves at a table in the outdoor dining section and watched sailboats in the distance gliding over the calm water of Long Island sound. As we ordered lunch, a Frank Sinatra impersonator began singing. We were tired, sweaty, and hungry, and it felt great to take a break from riding and enjoy the idyllic surroundings and the soothing music. Halfway through our lunch, "Sinatra" turned it up a bit, and when he launched into Jimmy Buffett's *Margaritaville*, Coleman and I simultaneously looked up. "What???" We were both huge Buffett fans, and this was the weirdest rendition of *Margaritaville* either of us had ever heard.

Coleman yelled across the table, "Jimbo, we gotta dance to this one!"

We jumped up and made our way onto the lawn. Steph and Dave followed. The four of us danced on the grass and tried to help "Sinatra" sing Jimmy Buffett. At one point, I saw Coleman trying to twirl Dave. Stephanie looked horrified—probably afraid that Coleman might knock Dave over or spin him into a tree. Dave had a big grin on his face. I couldn't help but laugh at the crazy scene. It was liberating to feel so carefree and light-hearted.

Right before I dozed off, my wandering mind took me to Vietnam. I pictured a young Dave with his five Ranger teammates dragging their bulky gear across the helicopter pad. As they carefully stepped over the skids and pushed their supplies into the belly of their Huey, they nervously teased one another, a pack of brothers giving each other shit to take the edge off. I envisioned the six of them standing there, laughing with each other, unaware that this would be their final mission together.

I fell asleep with that visual and Bob Dylan's words echoing in my brain: *"Knock, knock, knockin' on heaven's door..."*

CHAPTER 17
Riding for Ray

Day 2 (Labor Day, Monday, September 5, 2016)

I woke up Monday morning feeling well-rested. The four of us met downstairs in the common area of the hotel. Dave appeared in good spirits, completely recovered from the previous day's ride. Now that we were on the road, he seemed more comfortable opening up and reliving the past. As we sipped our coffees, he spoke decisively and told us about Ray Apellido, his assistant team leader. We would be riding for Ray today.

Ray was from Bakersfield, California. At 29 years of age, he was the venerable "grandfather" of Dave's Ranger team. During his six months in Vietnam, he had completed several missions. He could be demanding, but he was also quick with a smile or supportive pat on the back. Ray unofficially served as the "big brother" to all the younger guys around him, many of whom outranked him. Dave felt blessed to have him as a teammate and described him as "a man whose fierce appearance in the jungle belied a gentle soul."

Day two was one of my favorite days of biking. Over mostly flat terrain, we rode through suburbia—cookie cutter neighborhoods, small villages, quintessential America. We passed schools, churches, all types of homes, small businesses, family restaurants, parks, and playing fields. People of all ages were out and about, and everyone seemed happy to see us, smiling or waving as we cruised by. Those we talked to were supportive of our mission and offered prayers and words of encouragement.

In the early afternoon, we rode through a neighborhood that had flags mounted every 50-100 feet on telephone poles. They seemed to stretch for miles, the flags just touching the tops of our heads as we passed under. We felt certain they had been hung especially for us, to honor the men for whom we were riding.

During one particular split, Stephanie, Coleman, and I were riding. Coleman was in the lead and Steph in the rear, each of us spaced about ten feet apart. Our patriotic spirits were soaring, the three of us feeling like we were making our own grand parade. Steph had her phone out, and I briefly glanced back and yelled at her to take some video of all the flags. When I turned back around, I almost collided with Coleman. He had stopped to retrieve a small American flag that someone had dropped next to the road. I swerved around him, braking furiously as I ran up onto a freshly mowed lawn into a flower bed. Steph's view was blocked by me, and she followed in my tracks, also narrowly avoiding Coleman. Steph and I walked our bikes back to where Coleman stood, a bit irritated with him and also worried that the homeowner was going to run out and scold us for scuffing up the lush grass and crushing several flowers. Coleman displayed no concern that he had almost caused a three-bike pile-up. He pulled a bungie cord from his pack and carefully rigged the small flag so that it stood securely off the rear of his bike. For the rest of the ride, that little flag waved proudly.

In the suburbs closer to New York City, the roads became less bike-friendly and more congested. Some had no shoulder, and we realized riding conditions were too treacherous to continue onward. We decided to backtrack to the Cold Spring Harbor Rail Station and catch the commuter train from there into Penn Station. In Manhattan, we planned to bike to Pier 11 near Wall Street and catch a ferry to Highland, New Jersey.

I trusted our navigators, Coleman and Stephanie, who were often huddled over their phones, mumbling, sometimes disagreeing, and occasionally arguing. I had faith they would get us to our destinations, and they always did.

At the train station in Cold Spring Harbor, we said goodbye to Stephanie. She had volunteered to drive the car around New York City. As Dave, Coleman, and I boarded the train with our bikes, we glanced back over our shoulders and watched the taillights of the Subaru fade into the distance. After only two days together, it felt unsettling to be without one of our teammates.

It seemed surreal to be on a train with people going about their mundane routines while we were on such an unusual voyage. Together, the three of us stood with our bikes, lost in thought. The hypnotic rhythm of the rails blocked out surrounding noise, and my mind wandered. I remember feeling like I was "different" from all the "normal" people sitting around me. In my mind, I was a traveler on an epic quest. I likened my bike to a Viking ship, carrying me to places uncharted along a route yet to be determined, unveiling mysteries unknown. My reverie ended as the train began braking and pulled into Penn Station. I couldn't help but laugh at myself.

When the train doors opened, the three of us hoisted our bikes, disembarked, and climbed the stairs to street level. As we exited the train station, we were overwhelmed by city noises and masses of people. We slowly walked our bikes on a packed New York City sidewalk. After a few feet, we stopped, took in the surroundings, looked at each other, and smiled. We anticipated biking through Manhattan would be one of the highlights of the trip.

We eventually got our bearings and, with Coleman navigating, carefully started off. We followed a five-mile course that weaved from mid-town to lower Manhattan. Riding in the city was challenging with constant horns, traffic lights, and people everywhere. It took an hour to negotiate what felt like an obstacle course with seemingly hidden dangers lurking at every street corner. When we arrived at Pier 11, we could see the Brooklyn Bridge behind us and the expansive harbor ahead.

We had twenty minutes until our scheduled departure, so we jumped back onto our bikes and set off to find the Bull on Wall Street, which was only a few blocks over. The pedestrian traffic was so thick we had to walk our bikes. We turned a corner, and there it was, the iconic Bull, symbol of American capitalism. After taking a few selfies, we hurried back to the ferry dock, arriving without a second to spare. We barreled down the dock, yelling at the crew to wait. The ferry workers, clearly annoyed, frowned at us as we ran our bikes onto the boat. They immediately cast off.

The afternoon was still sunny with temperatures in the seventies and little wind. As the boat pulled away from the dock into the harbor, we saw Ellis Island and the Statue of Liberty off to our right. We were invigorated after our ride through the city, feeling fortunate to have experienced the vibe of the "Big Apple" on bikes. The three of us gazed back at lower Manhattan fading into the distance. I wished I could preserve that moment and slow down time. I felt like a character in an adventure novel, and I didn't want to turn the page.

We stayed outside on the top deck and snapped pictures as the boat plowed southward. After twenty minutes or so, we passed under the Verrazano-Narrows Bridge that connects Brooklyn with Staten Island, and in front of us, the New Jersey shoreline gradually came into view. When we arrived at the ferry dock, Stephanie was there with the car, happy (and I think relieved) that we had survived the bustle of NYC. We were glad to see her, our team reunited.

The ride from Highland to Red Bank, New Jersey, the location of our second day's lodging, was breathtaking. It began with a meandering bike path along a sparkling bay; then a winding, hilly road that passed gorgeous multi-million-dollar estates, horse stables, orchards, small farms, and lush gardens. At one point, Stephanie stopped in the middle of the road. With both arms raised, she slowly turned and said, "Jimmy. Stop! Look around you." I got off my bike and did a 360 taking in the stunning scenery that surrounded us, our senses overwhelmed by the natural and man-made beauty.

About six miles into the ride, Stephanie's rear derailleur broke, splitting in two. We pulled onto thick grass outside the gates of a huge mansion and rigged her chain so it would remain in place, but Stephanie was unable to shift gears. We limped the last four miles and coasted down a final hill into Red Bank.

Our hotel was located at the head of a wide harbor. Our rooms were on an upper floor, both with sweeping views over the water to the east, especially striking in the glow of the clear pre-dusk light. The four of us congregated in Coleman's and my room, and we sipped a glass of wine as we enjoyed the end of what had been an exceptional day. The water outside our windows had a golden-orange hue to it from the setting sun, and we watched the twinkling lights of boats returning as dusk turned to darkness. We toasted Ray one last time and then turned in. We were in bed by 9 pm.

I reviewed the day's events in my mind as I fell asleep. We had experienced the magic of cycling and the unexpected gifts bestowed upon the rider: the ability to slow down, appreciate the moment, and connect with ever changing surroundings. I had not anticipated how rewarding our mission on bikes would feel—the four of us supporting each other, laughing along the way, but also emotionally connecting with our Army Ranger heroes, all accentuated by the burn of our effort.

I smiled as I reflected back on some of the day's juvenile behavior. We had definitely reverted a bit with profanity now an integral descriptor in any conversation. Nothing could be described as just amazing. It was f'ing amazing. It was as if we had shed our previous personas and instead viewed ourselves as bad-ass Harley derelicts or delinquent teens on bicycles, obnoxiously assuming we owned the road. "Out of our way! We are coming through, four delusional riders with some very important cargo—the spirits of Harold and Ray. And we are gonna be pickin' up others as we continue south…SO DON'T MESS WITH US!"

CHAPTER 18
Riding for Anthony

Day 3 (Tuesday, September 6, 2016)

I awoke before 7 am, my eyes greeted by a stunning blue sky outside the hotel windows and a bright rising sun sparkling off the harbor water below. I didn't know it at this early hour, but the day was going to offer another defining ride. It would also be a day of discovery. Dave would inform us that the morning of September 20, 1970 in Vietnam claimed more lives than we had originally thought. His revelations would force us to abandon our plan to honor a single man each day.

We met at the hotel restaurant for breakfast and found a table outside overlooking the harbor. After we ordered coffee, Dave gave us our morning briefing. Today's ride would honor Anthony (Tony) Gallina. Tony was from Maplewood, Missouri. He was eighteen years old, the only team member younger than Dave. He had arrived in-country about the same time as Dave, and like Dave, he immediately volunteered for Ranger training. Tony had a handsome, boyish face and a youthful spirit. Shortly after entering base camp, a dog wandered out of the jungle and began following him. Tony adopted the dog and named him Roscoe. Legend had it that Roscoe could sniff out a Viet Cong from the hundreds of Vietnamese civilians who passed through the Army camp each day.

As Dave spoke, he reminded me of someone proudly bragging about a younger brother or son. I sensed he felt a special kinship with Tony and also, that he was reconnecting with all these guys. Each morning, I saw the pain in his eyes as he spoke of his teammates. But I also increasingly sensed fondness as he remembered these young men and the roles they played in his life. I again wondered if, at times, the three of us might be pushing Dave too hard mentally; if, despite what seemed like an impenetrable shell, we risked cracking his defense mechanisms. We were taxing him to his physical limits too, and we needed to make sure the combination of physical and emotional challenges did not overwhelm his positive spirit. Thankfully, the beauty and joy of biking and the constant humor evoked by the antics of our undertaking and our juvenile behavior balanced the serious and sometimes painful aspects of our mission. I was determined to keep the mood light and find ways to make Dave laugh.

Because Stephanie's bike needed repair, she took the car to find a bike shop while Dave, Coleman, and I made our way to the Jersey Shore. We would maintain phone contact, and Stephanie would catch up with us after her bike was fixed.

Ironically, Hermine, a massive storm we'd worried about all week leading up to the ride, turned out to be a blessing. After heading out to sea south of Jersey, it had changed course and swerved back to shore, hitting the coast of New England. In so doing, it provided us with perfect weather and a powerful breeze blowing from the north. Riding along our southbound route proved even more enjoyable, the brisk wind like a hand on our backs gently pushing us onward.

We traveled through small towns following a southeasterly route. As we neared the ocean, I felt and smelled the salty air. We hoped to take a beachfront road or even the boardwalk straight south along the ocean.

About an hour into the ride, the roads were quiet and traffic light. I was in the lead, effortlessly sailing with the wind at my back. I slowed down and waited for Dave and Cole to pull alongside me.

I glanced over at the two of them and asked, "You guys believe in a higher power?"

Coleman replied, "Now Jimmy, don't go getting all philosophical on us."

I retorted, "Seriously. How do you explain the perfect riding conditions plus a twenty-knot tailwind pushing us along? It seems that there's a higher presence looking down, in approval of our mission."

Dave smiled. "I suppose you are right." He then turned serious and continued, "Y'know, in addition to my Army Ranger teammates, a four-man helicopter crew and two infantry soldiers also died that morning."

I stopped my bike. What? How had I not thought of this? For some reason, I had focused on Dave's Ranger team and forgotten about the helicopter crew. And, I had always pictured other Hueys diving in to rescue Dave. I had not considered that there might be forward infantry soldiers already on the ground in the vicinity of the crash rushing in to help.

I walked my bike forward to where Dave and Coleman had pulled over to wait for me. "Dave, six more guys died that morning? We need to honor all of them. They are equally part of your story."

With a pained expression, Dave looked at the two of us and said, "I know. I'm not sure why I haven't mentioned the other guys until now. I think traveling on the open road has allowed for some clarity; reminded me of all who were part of that terrible morning."

We slowly started pedaling, weighed down by the understanding of just how tragic that morning had been. In the matter of minutes, eleven young souls were lost forever. Clocks across the world had continued ticking, and, for billions of people, those minutes passed and were unremarkable...uneventful...forgotten. In that small patch of desolate jungle, time stopped—dreams interrupted, goals destroyed. Dates counted down were irrelevant; loved ones' existences shattered. And Dave had witnessed it all go down.

For miles we rode side by side reflecting on the new information. We would need to research these other soldiers and decide how we would honor them. With time, the warmth of the sun, the grandness of our surroundings, and the prospect of arriving at the ocean buoyed our spirits.

I looked over. "Dave, tell us more about Tony."

Dave replied. "Tony was a really nice, unassuming guy. He was solid as a rock, all muscle, very tough. He had just graduated from high school before shipping out. He was just a kid."

As we neared the beach, the wind intensified. I felt certain that "Someone" was looking out for us. "Men, I am quite sure that our friend on high is lending assistance." Dave and Coleman looked up at the sky, and this time, I think, at that moment, they both believed me. At times, the wind was so strong that we could coast without pedaling.

We eventually reached an access road adjacent to the beach. We stopped multiple times to take pictures of the sites and churning surf, often riding on the boardwalk which was barren mid-week and post season. We reached Asbury Park and snapped some memorable pictures in front of a lifeguard chair, documenting that we were on hallowed ground previously traversed by The Boss. Around noon we met up with Stephanie, and Dave volunteered to drive.

Steph, Cole, and I continued south along the ocean, each of us impressed with the uniqueness of the Jersey shore. I think Stephanie's description captured the essence of this day's ride best. It so happened that today was also Dave's birthday.

Facebook Post (Stephanie), Tuesday, September 6, 2016

I only rode this afternoon because of my bike needing repairs, but the ride was amazing. We went down the Jersey shore along the boardwalk. Amusement parks, mini golf courses, and arcades were all around us. Americana. There were a few people out and about, but it was obvious that the season was now over. I could almost sense the crowds that had departed just days earlier to return to work and school after a perfect summer.

The homes along the shore were breathtaking with tons of character. I couldn't help but wonder what the fortunate souls who owned them did for a living.

During the past two days of riding, I've focused more on staying alive and less on the beauty of my surroundings and how fortunate I am to have the capacity to do this ride. Today, while riding, I reflected on what a huge sacrifice Dave, his teammates, and everyone who fights for this country made and continue to make.

At around 2 pm we decided to break for lunch. We found a crab shack situated at the end of a pier jutting out from the boardwalk. We parked our bikes and found an open table. As I walked, my upper legs felt tight and sore, but all other parts of me, from head to toe, remained primed to ride. It was empowering to realize that the further I biked, the stronger I got. Stephanie was right. We were blessed to have the capacity to do this.

We ate lunch outside and enjoyed the strong ocean breeze and the sound of waves crashing against the pilings underneath us.

We chugged down several glasses of water and ordered a round of ice-cold beers.

Looking at maps on our phones, we realized that the shore was about to become a thin barrier island separated from the mainland by a large protected bay. This radical spit of coastline took its name from the original Dutch settlers who had landed here centuries ago: Barnegat—inlet of the breakers, still impassable by road.

We decided we'd bike to the north side of the inlet. We would then load our bikes onto the car, backtrack, and drive off the barrier island, around Barnegat Bay, and then access the beach road south of the inlet and drive north to Barnegat Light, the resort town on the south side of the inlet. We knew that there was a historic lighthouse from which Barnegat Light took its name. It sounded like a cool place to spend the night.

just as we arrived at the southernmost point where forward progress became impossible by bike, the weather turned cloudy and a light drizzle began to fall. The timing and plan worked out perfectly. We loaded our bikes onto the car, backtracked up the coastal road, headed westward around the bay, made our way back to the shore, and then drove north into Barnegat Light.

The town seemed relatively deserted post-season, and there were fewer options for lodging than we expected. We eventually found two rooms at a retro style, low-priced motel. As we pulled into the parking area, the rain became steady. We left our bikes on the car and ran to our rooms.

Our friend Mike Denci, who we had last seen presiding over a prayer in our kitchen the morning of our departure, was in New Jersey on business. He wanted to meet up with us to celebrate Dave's birthday, so we planned a rendezvous at 7 pm at a seafood bar and restaurant a few blocks from our motel. As we showered and relaxed pre-meal in our quaint rooms, it poured outside. I checked my phone as Coleman typed away on my iPad.

Facebook Post (Coleman) Tuesday, September 6, 2016

When Jimmy first proposed this trip, I thought of it as an adventure. Well, more like a bad idea most surely destined to fail! As time rolled by and enthusiasm rose, I came to better understand Dave's desire to honor friends he bonded with over forty years ago. Life is a challenge, and rising to overcome obstacles, even hair-brained ideas proposed by Jimmy, pushes one to reach within. And in this case, possibly leaves one with some great memories. That's why I am here. War is an ugly thing. Young men and now women selflessly place themselves in harm's way. Dave's Ranger teammates, the four helicopter crewmen, and the troops sent in to secure the area perished that fateful day. They, as well as countless others, deserve our gratitude. Their memory should not die.

Before dinner, I e-mailed Andy to fill him in on the day's conversation and the fact that there were additional casualties in addition to Dave's teammates. Andy promised to investigate and communicate his findings by the next day.

At 6:45 pm, the four of us ventured outside and sprinted through the driving rain to our dining destination. By the time we reached the restaurant, we were cold and wet. We scored five seats at the end of the bar near a blazing fire. Shortly after sitting down, Mike burst through the door with a big smile on his face, happy to see us and eager to discover how we were making out. He was surprised that we appeared so upbeat. He admitted he had expected to find us beaten down by our miles on the road.

After dinner, we sang Happy Birthday to Dave. We then updated Mike on some of the highlights and more humorous moments of the ride. We also reviewed some of the information Dave had shared with us earlier that day. We would need to learn the names of all the men involved that morning in Vietnam, and, on the remaining days, ride for multiple men. We decided we would devote the next day to the helicopter crew.

By 9 pm, we were yawning, ready to turn in. Mike said good-bye, and the four of us walked back to our motel. The rain had stopped, but it was misty and chilly outside. We were exhausted, and within minutes of crawling into my bed, I fell soundly asleep.

CHAPTER 19
Riding for the Helicopter Crew

Day 4 (Wednesday, September 7, 2016)

awoke, dressed, and met the other three outside our adjacent rooms. The morning sky was gray with low-lying fog and intermittent light drizzle. We unloaded our bikes from the car and rode a few blocks to a deli that was open for breakfast. As we sat around a wobbly, wooden table and ate freshly made breakfast sandwiches, I shared an e-mail Andy had sent the night before:

Hi, Jim. If you have not read this, here is a link to the Prologue of a book named The Price of Exit *by Tom Marshall. The prologue tells part of Dave's story of 9/20/70. It's tough to read knowing Dave and realizing the pain and mixed emotions he has endured over the past forty years.*

I have been reading your Facebook posts and saw the one from yesterday. Unfortunately, yes, you have your math right: 11 KIA.

Your posts have shared some incredible insight. They have been very enjoyable and enlightening reading. Please keep them coming.

Dave is the definition of a True Hero. Not just because he served in war; but because he lives a life that all of us should try to emulate. No adversity stops him. He keeps moving forward, no matter what is dealt to him. He never complains or looks for sympathy. He perpetually explores life, shares it, has a genuine interest in everyone he meets, and he gives and gives and gives, always in a generous spirit of joy. What a role model for all!

After reading Andy's e-mail to the others, Dave revealed what he knew of the four guys who made up the helicopter crew: 1Lt. Albert M. Finn, WO1 Larry G. Baldwin, crew chief SGT Dan O. Felts, and gunner SGT William T. Dotson III. They ranged in age from 20 to 26 years and were from Pennsylvania, Alabama, Arizona, and Texas respectively. We collectively echoed each man's name and looked at their pictures. We felt a strong attachment to the men we rode for each day.

After breakfast, we biked the short distance to the lighthouse perched on the south side of the narrow inlet and took pictures and wandered onto the jetty. Huge swells broke against the rocks, I presumed the aftermath of Hermine.

I was designated car driver for the first leg of the day's ride. Before leaving, Coleman showed me the route they tentatively planned to take. As soon as they crossed the bridge from the barrier island making up this part of the Jersey shore, they planned to ride southwest through some small neighborhoods before eventually intersecting Route 9, the road that would take us around some bays and then back to the shore further south into Atlantic City. I figured I would drive the car directly to Route 9, head south, and find a spot to pull over and wait for them to make the first exchange of driving. This would give the three of them fifteen miles or so, a little more than the usual split, which was fair because I'd taken the fewest driving shifts up to that point.

Stephanie, Dave, and Coleman started off on their bikes, and I watched them slowly fade into the mist. I lazily packed up our gear. I then briefly FaceTimed my sister Evie, who was with my mom. My mom seemed very happy when I told her what I was doing, mostly because she could sense I was having so much fun. At that time, she was in the later stages of dementia, but she still knew who I was. Her closing comment was, "Now Jimmy, you be careful."

I smiled. Sometimes, despite dementia, her motherly instincts still shone through. I thought back to a few weeks earlier when I had visited her with three of my siblings. We sat in her small assisted living apartment gossiping and catching up on each other's recent exploits. My mom could not follow the conversation, though she pretended to understand and tried her hardest to stay engaged. At one point, my sister Evie said *"shit,"* and my mother immediately interrupted us to scold Evie on her choice of words. Certain things still broke through and rekindled her memory—in that case what was proper language and what wasn't.

I loaded up the car and then drove the proposed route. Several miles after turning south on Route 9, I pulled into a bank parking lot. The fog had burned off, and the sky was mostly clear except for random wafting clouds. Most of the puddles from the previous day's rain had vanished. Absent-mindedly, I walked over the thick lawn in front of the bank and sat down adjacent to the shoulder of the road, expecting the imminent arrival of my fellow travelers. I drank a bottled water as I waited…and waited…and waited.

I began to wonder if my teammates had ridden beyond where I was situated, but I deduced that was impossible. I tried to call and FaceTime Stephanie, but despite multiple attempts, no answer. I moved under a tree, leaned back, and clicked the link Andy had sent me to the Prologue of Tom Marshall's *"The Price of Exit."* I carefully read the words on the pages in front of me, periodically glancing up, expecting to see Dave, Stephanie, and Coleman riding toward me.

Prologue

Sunday, September 20, 1970
Quang Tri, I Corps, Republic of Vietnam

The Phoenix was Company C (Assault Helicopters), 158th Aviation Battalion, 101st Airborne Division (Air-mobile). It was based at Camp Evans, midway between Hue (pronounced "way") to the south and the demilitarized zone separating North and South Vietnam.

The morning of September 20, 1970 started like any other mission day. Rising before dawn, they departed the Phoenix Nest at oh-dark-thirty, to fly another combat assault. They would be carrying Army Rangers, supporting troops of the 1st Brigade of the 5th Mechanized Infantry Division. The 1/5 was dispersed along the Northern border with the enemy, North Vietnam. The intended landing zone was on the north side of the demilitarized zone, where the NVA didn't expect them. The Huey helicopter departed the Phoenix Nest at Camp Evans and proceeded north to Quang Tri.

*At the 1/5 Mechanized Infantry pad, Papa Company Rangers assembled. Killer team 1-8 boarded the Phoenix Huey. Sgt. Harold Sides, from Dallas, Texas, was the team leader. With him were Sp4. Raymond Apellido, the assistant team leader, of Bakersfield, California. Sp4. Dale Gray and another Ranger (**Dave**) took their positions, sitting in the door of the Huey's cargo bay, with their feet dangling over the helicopter skids. Team members Sp4. Anthony Gallina of Maplewood, Missouri, and PFC Glenn Ritchie of Mount Pleasant, North Carolina, also assumed their positions. They were well trained and highly experienced. They were to spend six days setting ambushes and booby traps near the center of the demilitarized zone, an eight-mile-wide swath stretching from the South China Sea to the Laotian border.*

With the Rangers loaded, the Huey departed Quang Tri, climbing to an altitude of only one hundred feet. Across the panoramic landscape of Quang Tri Province, the South China Sea was visible two miles to the east. The beautiful but deadly mountains of North Vietnam and Laos filled a distant horizon to the northwest. Flying high above them was the command-and-control Huey. It was accompanied by a Cobra gunship light-fire team, two Cobras ready to dive at the slightest provocation to the Huey.

It was a classic assault helicopter operation—inserting Rangers behind enemy lines. The Rangers' intent was to place mines and booby traps, perhaps capture a prisoner. Then to kill as many of the enemy as possible—creating havoc and fear, disrupting the enemy's daily routine on his home turf.

Passing west of Dong Ha, the last South Vietnamese village and military base, they descended to twenty or so feet above the ground, below the enemy radar horizon. Continuing northwest, they passed just west of Con Then, the site of major battles between U.S. Marines and the NVA during the mid 1960s.

First Lieutenant Al Finn, the Phoenix 1st Platoon leader, was the aircraft commander. He was flying with a young warrant officer as his copilot. Passing west of Outpost Charlie-Two, which overlooked the demilitarized zone, they descended to five to ten feet above ground. Accelerating to one hundred knots airspeed, the Huey entered the DMZ at an altitude of less than ten feet with a speed approaching 120 miles per hour. It was a demanding ground-level sprint across the barren mudscape. The view was reminiscent of a World War I no-man's land. The exit would also be as fast and as low as the Huey could go; North Vietnamese bunkers with .51-caliber anti-aircraft machine guns were dispersed throughout the area. Flying even fifty feet above ground level would assure death at the hands of NVA .51s.

For the young Rangers, the Huey helicopter was a magic-carpet ride. With their feet dangling above the skids, they looked into the onrushing air, intently observing their objective. Flying at 120 miles per hour a few feet above the ground was quite a rush.

The Huey was coming loud and mean. The whopping of the rotor blades in normal flight was casual compared to sounds of the assaulting Huey. Its speed did not compare to that of an airplane. But in the three-mile-an-hour world of an infantryman, 120 miles per hour at five to ten feet above the ground was awesome.

The North Vietnamese could hear the helicopter coming two miles away, less than a minute's flight time, but the sound from ground-level flight was diffused enough to mask the Huey's east location and direction. An NVA gunner alert enough to hear it coming would have to be quick and lucky to get a killing shot at the Americans.

The crew chief, Sp4 Dan Felts, and gunner, Sp4 William Dotson, scanned the onrushing landscape. They were flexing their M-60 machine guns, cleared hot, ready to suppress enemy fire.

The mission risk was high, but it was accepted as their duty. The aircrew, as well as the Rangers, believed it would be a routine killer-team insertion. The Phoenix had done it successfully many, many times before. Just another day in the saddle.

Suddenly, the Huey nosed into the ground, flipping tail over nose into a flaming mass. In an instant, four helicopter crew members and five Rangers died. Badly injured, one Ranger was thrown from the aircraft……"

Wow! There it was, right in front of me—detailed and different from what I had imagined. No hovering; no time to anticipate the crash. Over 100 mph. Instant death. Yet somehow Dave had survived. I felt a disquieting weight in the pit of my stomach, as if I had witnessed a terrible catastrophe with my own eyes. I contemplated life, and death, and the thin line, in this case less than a second, separating the two.

When I looked up from my phone, I saw Dave, Stephanie, and Coleman riding single file along the road's shoulder. I waited until they pulled up to me, and then with an annoyed tone, I asked, "Where in the hell have you guys been?"

Stephanie looked exasperated. She responded, "You know those neighborhoods Coleman was convinced would intersect Route 9? Well, the neighborhoods ended in dirt roads which then led into a swamp. We dragged our bikes around the swamp, through dense woods, blazing our own trail. We finally connected with a dirt road which did eventually intersect a paved road and finally hooked up with Route 9. Where have we been? We've been following Coleman to hell and back because COLEMAN IS ALWAYS RIGHT."

Coleman shrugged his shoulders, and with a defeated look on his face remained silent.

Dave walked over and showed me pictures of the three of them carrying their bikes through water and over thick fallen tree trunks. He looked up at me and smiled. "You picked the right leg to drive."

I laughed. "I've been trying to call and FaceTime you guys for the last hour. You must have been completely off the grid. What an adventure!"

The four of us walked over to the car, and I handed each of them a bottled water from the cooler. We then sprawled out on the green grass. As cars sped by, I listened with amusement as the three of them relayed details of their back-country adventure. I couldn't help but laugh, and soon all four of us were rolling in the grass laughing at and with each other. I then updated Dave, Stephanie, and Coleman about what I had read in Marshall's *The Price of Exit*. As I spoke, I watched Dave's face, but he registered no surprise. I think all the details I described were already in his head.

I continued, "Andy said two support soldiers died in the ensuing firefight, but I don't know if they came in by helicopter or were part of Army Infantry already on the ground nearby, called in once the crash occurred."

189

Dave frowned. "It was forward Army Infantry already in the area, at least a few guys close enough to converge on the crash site within five to ten minutes or less. It was my superior officers in the command helicopter that came in and picked me up, but the infantry guys secured the crash site."

I hoped Andy would clarify that there were no more than two additional men killed in action.

We stood up and stretched. Dave was tired and clearly uncomfortable, so he volunteered to drive the next leg. Stephanie, Coleman, and I jumped onto our bikes and continued following Route 9 southwest, away from the Jersey shore. We pushed hard for two hours. In areas with heavy traffic, we tried to find roads adjacent to Route 9 more amenable to biking, but our phone maps repeatedly led us astray. We traveled down lightly paved forest fire access roads, many that looked promising on the map but, in fact, led nowhere. On one, we passed for three miles through a thick pine forest before realizing it was a dead end and doubling back.

At about 1 pm, we met up with Dave at a dining establishment on the Mullica River, seemingly in the middle of nowhere. As we ate lunch, we studied the map and realized that after another few miles, Route 9 became the Garden State Parkway, a major interstate highway impossible to bike, which would make cycling from our lunch location back to the Jersey shore impossible.

We decided we would drive the twelve to thirteen miles of the Garden State Parkway that wrapped around Reeds and Absecon Bays before heading closer to the coast near the outskirts of Atlantic City. Stephanie's legs were tired, and it was her turn to drive. She agreed to drop us outside Atlantic City so Dave, Coleman, and I could cycle past the casinos and enjoy the boardwalk leading south through other small seaside towns before crossing a series of bridges into Ocean City. I was excited to visit Ocean City. My college friend Pete had grown up there, and I had several preconceived images in my head of his hometown based on multiple late-night conversations I'd had with him years ago.

The four of us loaded our bikes onto the car. Stephanie drove and I rode shotgun. I thought back to the passage from *The Price of Exit*. I pictured a younger Dave with his war paint on, sitting with his feet hanging out over the skids of the Huey as the world flashed by. I envisioned the other nine young men confined in the small belly of their flying machine. I imagined their sharpened senses, the deafening roar, the hot jungle air blowing in their faces. It must have been terrifying and exhilarating at the same time. Given the speed and manner of approach, it seemed impossible to me that anyone could survive a sudden crash.

Upon entering the outskirts of Atlantic City, Stephanie pulled over and dropped the three of us. She planned to continue south to Ocean City, find a place to park, put her feet up, and take a nap. We told her we would text her as we entered Ocean City.

It was interesting riding bikes through Atlantic City. We passed large casinos and giant hotels next to crumbling homes and other run-down buildings. There was a palpable feeling of the ocean, big money, and seediness all rolled into one: new and old; rich and poor. As I pedaled, the refrain from Bruce Springsteen's song *Atlantic City* played over and over in my head – "Meet me tonight, in Atlantic City." I could sense the vibe riding on bikes.

South of town, we coasted onto the boardwalk and rode for miles along the ocean with the wind still at our backs. As the afternoon progressed, the wind gradually died, the ocean calmed, and the temperature and humidity increased.

Several miles south of Atlantic City we rode into Margate and came upon Lucy the Elephant, a six-story novelty building in the shape of a massive elephant. I immediately thought of my older daughter Meg who was teaching in Thailand for the year. Six months earlier, she had finished a two-month internship at an orphanage for elephants, her favorite animal. She had lived with and helped care for a group of domesticated elephants that had been rescued with their mahouts (trainers) from performing on the crowded, dirty streets of Thailand's major cities. I stopped and took a picture of the odd building, and I texted it to Meg. Given the time difference, I did not expect to hear back from her.

A few miles further south we encountered the bridges leading into Ocean City. it was a stunning afternoon—clear blue skies and, from atop the bridges, a panoramic view as we looked southeasterly over Ocean City. We continued off the second bridge and made our way back to the shore and again picked up the boardwalk. We coasted parallel to the ocean through the main part of town and enjoyed the sight of the shimmering beach leading down to the clear water of the Atlantic. Ocean City, self-proclaimed "America's Family City," at least superficially appeared to live up to its name—a wholesome, perfectly manicured, little piece of paradise.

South of the main boardwalk area, we continued riding through scenic beachfront neighborhoods that seemed to stretch endlessly along the coast. Traffic was light on the beach road, and we pedaled next to each other, engaged in lively conversation. We drifted back to the morning in Vietnam.

I asked Dave if he knew the name of the lieutenant who supervised his insertion and then dove in with the command and control helicopter to pull him out.

Dave nodded his head. "Yes, Lieutenant Roger Bergh."

I inquired, "Do you know what happened to him?"

Dave began answering, but then paused. After a few seconds, he replied, "No. I've had no contact with him since that morning."

I could tell Dave's mind was spinning. I suspected he was thinking about Lieutenant Bergh and wanted to say more, but he remained quiet. I didn't push him.

We had tried communicating with Stephanie several times but were unsuccessful. We finally caught up with her a few miles south of Ocean City. A large bridge led out of town into Strathmere, and we stopped at an inn just off the bridge. It had been one of my friend Pete's favorite watering holes during summers home from college, and I wanted to take a picture there to text to him. It was now past 4 pm. Hot, sweaty, and exhausted, we decided to go in and enjoy a drink in Pete's honor. We mingled with the locals as we slowly sipped ice-cold beers. We looked at maps on our phones and decided we would continue south for another twenty miles and spend the night in Stone Harbor. We called ahead and made a reservation for two rooms at a hotel in the middle of town.

Dave, Steph, and Coleman decided to drive there. They were physically and emotionally drained. I still felt energized and wanted to continue riding. The other three mounted their bikes onto the rack and drove off. I watched the car fade into the distance and then continued south along the ocean.

After the camaraderie of riding together for the past four days, it felt lonely to be on the road by myself. But it was a gorgeous evening, and I felt compelled to continue onward. By this time, we had adopted a mindset that if one person was riding, we were all on the road. One for all and all for one—we were a team.

I passed through small beachfront enclaves broken up by estuaries, public beaches, and undeveloped seaside wilderness. There was water on both sides of the road, the Atlantic Ocean on my left and a large bay on my right. Traffic was light, and in some places, thick seagrass and tall reeds blocked my views on both sides of the road. The air was warm as the sun descended and the western sky became multicolored.

As I rode, I felt solitary and introspective. Memories of my dad and Arlan popped into my mind. I imagined how much my dad would have enjoyed meeting Dave and sharing stories. And how Arlan would have instantly fit into our group, riding with purpose, probing into a mystery, and then relaxing and laughing over a few beers. I looked up at the sky, a blend of pink, orange, and yellow hues, and I felt the presence of the two of them, a certainty in my gut that they approved of our mission and were proud of Stephanie, Dave, Coleman, and me for taking this trip on. I pictured my dad shaking his head in the affirmative, acknowledging that I was finally playing that "perfect game" he always knew I had in me.

My daughter Meg FaceTimed me from Thailand, and with my phone in its holder on the handlebars of my bike, I spoke with her for thirty minutes as I continued pedaling. Seeing her face and hearing her voice from half a world away added to the euphoria of completing another day's ride. There must have been "family support karma" in the air because as soon as I hung up with Meg, my other daughter, Kate, FaceTimed to check in.

As I finished updating Kate, dusk faded rapidly, and I worried I might not reach my destination before dark. My cell phone was dying, and I was dependent on it for navigation. I picked up the pace and powered in for the final six miles, arriving at the hotel entrance just as darkness blanketed Stone Harbor and my phone died. The four of us had covered over eighty miles on a perfect day, one that I didn't want to end.

When I entered the hotel room, I discovered that Coleman had again done laundry. I found a pile of clean clothes, including underwear neatly folded at the end of my bed. I marveled at his multi-dimensional talents. Under his rough exterior, there was clearly a guy who took on whatever task was necessary. I finally understood how his lovely wife, Linda, tolerated him.

Over dinner, we looked at the map and planned the next morning's route. Coleman volunteered to drive. The other three of us planned to bike the twenty miles to the Cape May Ferry dock to catch a boat that would transport us across Delaware Bay, from New Jersey to Delaware. Our morning's route would lead us inland, away from the beach, this time for the remainder of the trip.

After dinner, we casually strolled through town, enjoying the beauty of Stone Harbor and the salty sea breeze. When we returned to our rooms, the others immediately fell asleep. Despite aching muscles and a deep, total body fatigue, I was unwilling to give up on the day. I couldn't sleep, so I posted on Facebook.

Facebook Post (Jim) Wednesday, September 7, 2016

…Though he didn't know the Huey crew members well, Dave had the highest respect and regard for them. He told us they were legendary for taking great risks to get their precious cargo of Army Rangers safely off-board and, during pick-ups, out of harm's way. He became especially saddened this morning as we talked about their tragic deaths that day in the jungle. Equally hard for Dave, I think, was the thought of the support team coming in and taking two more casualties to get him and the bodies of his friends out. Hard enough to lose five fighting brothers. The other guys were collateral damage from things gone badly wrong that morning. This was not their mission.

Some of you reading my daily posts have asked about tracking down some of the key players in this saga, for instance, the Lieutenant who took the command Huey in and found Dave. I shouldn't speak for him, but I think Dave would like that person (whose name we know) to understand that he (Dave) has lived an honorable life, that it was worth the risk he (the Lieutenant) took that day. But I don't know if it would be therapeutic or traumatic, expressing gratitude but at the same time bringing those events from long ago back into glaring focus. It's a fine balance. I feel some mornings we push Dave a little too hard for information. However, I also feel that our little group is doing our best to honor these guys, and we need vital information to connect with them. We talk about them all day, and by getting their stories out, their memory is celebrated. When we see their names on the Wall, they will certainly be more to us than just names. We will see their eternally young faces. We will talk to them, shed tears for them, and thank them…

It was after midnight when I finished typing. I tried to sleep, but I couldn't beat back an overwhelming emptiness as I thought about the multiple young men killed that morning 46 years ago. I sat up in bed and looked out the window at the moon lighting up the night sky.

I thought back to the sixties and remembered the fear I felt as a child when I watched the evening news with my parents or thumbed through the pages of *Life* magazine. Even as a preteen, I was fully aware that young American soldiers, many not much older than me, were coming back in body bags. I knew some of them had volunteered, but that a large percentage had been drafted and sent a half a world away with no say in the matter. I recalled lying in bed at night feeling unsettled, afraid that one day I, too, would be ordered to that steaming jungle to stare down an enemy and fight a war I didn't understand.

I also experienced firsthand how the draft impacted young college-aged students of that era. I remember riding the ferry back from our summer cottage in Ohio on a Sunday evening in late August before starting 5th grade. At the time, our island's interior was covered with rolling vineyards. There was a rustic old winery that served wine from the grapes harvested there, and on weekends the winery was packed with college students. Mostly, they would sit in small groups on a lawn that gently sloped down to the lake. Usually, the college kids were well behaved, but occasionally the mixture of excessive alcohol and youthful ebullience resulted in unruly behavior. On that particular boat ride, there were several inebriated young men, and my parents warned me to keep my distance.

Initially, I sat inside, but I became restless and decided to take a stroll around the boat. I gingerly walked around clusters of college kids and found some space hanging onto the outer railing looking over the edge of the boat. Next to me were four guys seated on the deck, all with their heads down. One of the guys looked up and pointed at me. "Hey, little dude, guess where I gotta one-way ticket to?"

His unsteady arm seemed to be reaching for me, and I instinctively moved further away. The young man was smoking a cigarette and had a second one, unlit, dangling out of his ear. His eyes were bloodshot and his words slurred. "My draft number got called. I'm heading to Viet.....nam." Even through the drunken stupor, I could sense his angst and uncertainty.

I must have appeared frightened, because he continued, "Hey little guy. I'm sorry if I scared you." With a resigned look on his face, he then stared back down at his feet. His friends remained silent. I backed away. When I was out of their sight, I ran to find my family. I didn't leave my parents' side for the rest of the ride. I wondered if that guy with the wavering arm and bloodshot eyes, would be another soldier coming home in a body bag.

I fell asleep picturing an unlit cigarette dangling from that college kid's ear from so many years ago.

CHAPTER 20
Riding for Richard and Michael

Day 5 (Thursday, September 8, 2016)

Despite having fallen asleep late the night before, I awoke before sunrise. Coleman was still sleeping, so I quietly sat up and opened Facebook on my phone. I was heartened and frankly amazed to see all the people who were following our ride, offering supportive comments, and sharing our posts. Friends from grade school, high school, college, and others I didn't even know weighed in.

Meg had taken a screen shot of our FaceTime session from the day before and posted it. Her post showed a picture of me, intently riding with her little head in the corner with the caption,

Happy to join this guy for a little bit of his ride from RI to D.C., though I was low-key worried I was going to witness him run into another curb. You rock Daddio!

Kate couldn't help but reply, *Hahaha, I had the same concern when I was Facetiming him.*

In addition to imagining my wipeout from day one of the ride (which I had described in a previous Facebook post both girls had read), my daughters probably also had memories from a few years previously when I had jumped onto my friend Mike's shiny new Harley, completely unaware of how heavy and difficult it was to maneuver when not powered. Next thing I knew, I slowly toppled over with the Harley landing on top of me. Unable to move or right the bike, Mike and my brother-in-law Bob had to pull the bike off me. Once they knew I was okay, my daughters laughed for hours.

My high school friend, Milane posted a picture of her bike with the caption:

Took little miss sunshine to the end of the road—Everglades National Park just past here. I love to ride my bike every day, but my new inspiration is my friend Jim Ziegler who is currently on the ride of a lifetime!!!! Be safe my friend.

Coleman stirred, and we walked downstairs to check on our bikes. It was steaming hot outside, the air heavy and still. We had lost our tailwind and would be heading away from the shore, so riding was going to be more challenging today.

As we re-entered the lobby, we ran into Steph and Dave, and the four of us took an early morning walk through town. We found a popular diner, sat down, and ordered breakfast. Over coffee, we looked at the map and decided on the day's route.

We had made a reservation on the 11 am ferry from Cape May to Lewes, Delaware the night before. After disembarking, we planned to make our way to Route 16, which by the map appeared to be a lesser traveled country road that wound through the rural heart of Delaware crossing over into Maryland. Our goal for the day was Denton, Maryland, about eighty miles southwest of where we sat.

I had received an e-mail from Andy before sunrise confirming what Dave knew. There had been a platoon of Army Infantry guys near the crash site, and a few of them arrived on scene within five minutes or so. Two of them died from enemy fire.

Andy sent us information on the two young men; I am not sure of its source. Today, we would ride for them. They were not part of the mission, but without hesitation, they selflessly rushed in to help. They were partly responsible for saving Dave.

"First Lieutenant Richard Stube hurried with others to secure the crash site and search for survivors. A friend described Richard as having a terrific sense of humor. He was the oldest of seven siblings, and he often talked about his family in Montana. He was married and had an 18-month-old daughter. He carried a family photo that he showed off any chance he got. He and his wife were expecting a second child at the time of his death.

Private First-class Michael Linville was from Madison Heights, Michigan. He was days away from marrying his high school sweetheart in Hawaii when he volunteered for a mission to rescue the crew and Rangers shot down in the DMZ on September 20, 1970. Michael was twenty years old. When he arrived on the scene, he rushed to the chopper which was burning and partially submerged in water. Like Richard, a direct hit from mortar fire killed him. Michael's goal was to become a policeman after the war, just like his father."

Together, the four of us looked at pictures and thought about these two men. We again contemplated the peripheral wreckage, near and far. When the mortar fire killed Stube and Linville, other members of their infantry team were nearby and tried to provide assistance. All efforts were to no avail. Their teammates watched helplessly as each man took his last breath in an unforgiving jungle thousands of miles from home. I'm sure some, like Dave, suffered deep guilt that they had survived, unscathed, while their dear friends had suffered such violent deaths. I couldn't fathom the unbearable anguish of family and friends when news reached home.

It was after 9 am when we exited the diner. Slowly and deliberately, we walked back to our hotel, deep in thought. It was sometimes an emotional challenge to recover from our morning briefings and recharge for the day's ride. We were becoming more deeply attached to the young men for whom we were riding. But we still had several miles of open road before us, and we couldn't lose sight of our primary objective—getting Dave safely to the Wall. We needed to regroup and continue onward.

Coleman fretted that we didn't have enough time to bike to the ferry dock. Stephanie, Dave, and I thought we should attempt to ride as far as possible and call Coleman for rescue if we were cutting it too close. Dave was valiantly fighting a severe case of chafing, but he wanted to try riding. He agreed that if he held us up, Coleman could grab him first.

We set off at 9:40 am heading west over a bridge from the barrier island to the mainland. After two days of spectacular riding conditions and scenery, we were sad to leave the New Jersey coast.

At about 10:20 am, we were still ten miles from the ferry landing. We met up with Coleman, and Dave secured his bike on the rack and jumped into the car. Stephanie and I continued pedaling furiously in a last-ditch attempt to sprint to our destination. Ten minutes later, we realized we were not going to make it. Coleman pulled up next to us and yelled out the window, "C'mon you knuckleheads. Get in the friggin' car. We are going to miss our boat."

Steph and I looked at each other and regrettably admitted that Coleman was right. We loaded our bikes onto the rack and hopped into the car for the final push. As soon as our doors closed,

Coleman gunned it, and we raced to the dock and pulled into the line of cars just as they finished loading onto the ferry.

The 85-minute ride across Delaware Bay turned out to be relaxing and fun. It made me think of our own Rhode Island jewel, Narragansett Bay, though the Delaware was clearly larger at its mouth than our Bay. There was no wind, and the water was dead calm with a haziness over the surface that limited visibility. We sat on the front deck for the first half hour and then walked to the rear deck for the remainder of the trip. We socialized with some of the other passengers. Everyone we spoke with supported our mission and ended conversations wishing us Godspeed.

The ride through Delaware into Maryland was tough. It was stifling hot and sticky. Thankfully, biking provides an ever-present breeze, but for the first time for me, riding felt like work. We were drenched in sweat and covered with a film of road grime.

The oppressive riding conditions added to my already overly inflated cycling ego. I now felt like I was riding against the devil in the heat of hell, determined to blast my way through no matter what he lobbed at me. Though aware of my responsibility for my fellow riders' safety, at times I felt invincible, as if my bike and I were unstoppable. I had never been on a trip like this before—the circumstances sometimes allowing my irrational side to completely nullify logic and reason. But then, this entire trip defied sound judgment. Many had told us we were crazy, and maybe each passing day pushed us a little closer to the edge.

We traveled over mostly flat, open farmland, occasionally passing through small towns. We stopped at several produce stands for fresh fruit, juice, and water refills. Given the weather conditions, It was difficult to maintain adequate hydration, and more than once, one of us got off his or her bike during a break and stumbled, almost toppling over. Thankfully, there was always a co-rider nearby to intercede and prevent a serious fall…except once. Shortly after entering Maryland, we pulled off the road into an abandoned gas station

202

for a water break. Coleman was looking a little peaked as he tried to dismount from his bike. I reached out and grabbed his arms but could only slow his collapse onto steaming hot blacktop. He laid prostrate on his back. Just as I was about to jump down to start administering CPR, Coleman began waving his arms like a snow angel, opened his eyes, and smiled. He slowly sat up, and after chugging a Gatorade, stood up and climbed onto his bike. We made our way back out to the road and continued onward.

Traffic was intermittently heavy, but there was a wide shoulder, so we felt safe. Making it to Denton seemed doable, so during a break in the later afternoon, we called ahead and booked a reservation at a Best Western Hotel. By 5 pm, we were only twenty-five miles away. We had traded driving shifts all day. As evening hit, it was Coleman's turn to drive. Dave decided he was done for the day, so he and Coleman drove ahead to check into the hotel. Stephanie and I continued riding through the rural landscape, past fields, family homesteads with charming farmhouses and outbuildings, and occasional commercial farming operations. As the sun began setting, we entered the outskirts of Denton, flew through town, and found our hotel.

I distinctly recall riding across the hotel parking lot, looking directly into the top crescent of the sun, its body almost completely below the tree line in front of us, the sky again ablaze with colors. Sweat, saturated with filth from car exhaust and dust from the open road, dripped off my face. Today had been about persevering, getting to our destination. Stephanie and I looked at one another and smiled. We shared a profound sense of accomplishment and immense pride as we coasted across the asphalt. We had achieved our goal in ninety-plus degree heat and air so sticky it clung to us and felt like a weight holding us back. Though my legs were a little unstable as I dismounted from my bike, it felt awesome limping through the entrance of the hotel into the air-conditioned lobby.

We stowed our bikes in our rooms and after cleaning up drove into the commercial center of Denton, Maryland. Once again, we found ourselves in a beautiful village—a place with history and charm. We parked the car and walked a few blocks, appreciating the sights and sounds of small-town America. We found an Irish pub in the middle of town. We chugged down several pitchers of ice water and filled up on Shepherd's Pie. While we ate, we looked at the map and realized we were only seventy miles from Washington, D.C. We were closing in.

After dinner, we drove back to the hotel. The other three went up to our rooms. I stayed in the lobby. I found a comfortable chair and sat with my legs up, thinking back on the events of the day. I opened Facebook on my iPad to compose an update and discovered that Dave had posted earlier that day, possibly during a driving break.

Facebook Post (Dave) Thursday, September 8, 2016

I am the luckiest person on earth. I am traveling with angels. My companions seem to have reached a secret agreement to protect me on our journey, to deliver me safely to the Wall by Saturday at noon. They gently steer me into the safest, middle position with one riding between me and the road. They coax me across busy intersections. They wait for me if I am slow climbing a hill. I am overwhelmed by the sacrifices each one has made to be here, the hours spent training, a week away from family, the cost of a new (or fixing up a) bike, the money spent on the trip, the vacation time sacrificed. Thank you for accompanying me on this final mission Steph, Jim, and Cole.

I contemplated Dave's post. I didn't feel that there was any self-sacrifice on my part. True, I was going to do whatever I could to get him safely to the Wall in D.C., but I felt blessed and honored to be a part of this mission. There was no place I would rather be.

CHAPTER 21
Riding for Glenn

Day 6 (Friday, September 9, 2016)

I woke up around 7 am, excited that by the day's end we would be just outside D.C. Coleman was already awake and showering. I sat in bed and opened Facebook. Stephanie had posted earlier:

Facebook Post (Stephanie) Friday morning, September 9, 2016

I blew out a flip-flop. For the third time in my life, I blew out a flip-flop. I grabbed a 15-year-old pair of Aldo flip-flops for this trip, I don't know why. The glue had failed, and with every step the sole was detaching, the decorative parts falling off. Last night at dinner the whole top detached from the sole. Aluminum foil and derma bond are currently holding it together. And Coleman thinks HE is MacGyver!

We are getting tired but hanging in there, working on a mystery, delving into Dave's Vietnam experience. Hopefully, we will get some answers for Dave before all is said and done. He deserves to know the truth about that day in September of 1970.

Today we will cross Chesapeake Bay (illegal to bike over, so we will go by car). This is a milestone for sure. We are almost there. My respect for and friendship with my teammates continues to grow with every mile. Dave is so lucky to have these guys as friends, and they are lucky to have him. We will always be like family, more so than we already were...

We had explored ways of crossing Chesapeake Bay the night before and found that there was a single bridge providing a direct path to Washington D.C.; it specifically forbid bicycles. Our only alternative was to cycle an extra hundred miles around the head of the Chesapeake and then circle back down to Washington, clearly not a workable plan. We decided to bike the thirty or so miles to land's end, and then drive across the Bay into Annapolis. From the map, there appeared to be a bike path closer to the Bay that crossed a few small islands before the large car-only bridge.

We met in the hotel lobby for a quick breakfast. Today's ride would be in memory of Glenn Ritchie, another of Dave's Ranger teammates. Glenn was a 19-year-old from Mount Pleasant, NC. He was planning on studying for the Lutheran ministry after his tour of duty ended. He had signed on for two years with the highest ideals, believing that all people, everywhere, deserved the same right to liberty that Americans enjoyed.

Those too young to remember the Cold War might feel such idealism was misplaced or reflective of American arrogance, an assumption that the "American system" was the best form of governance for all people everywhere. What such individuals don't understand is that communism, though egalitarian in concept, was (and still is) usually evil in practice. My parents' generation had watched

Russia overpower Eastern Europe after World War II. Formerly free countries installed militaristic regimes aligned with Moscow. Individuals were stripped of personal liberties, force fed propaganda, and held against their collective will. Walls were built, physically separating the masses from freedom, and travel outside the "iron curtain" was forbidden. The penalty for attempted escape was death.

I remember at fourteen years of age during a family trip to Europe, peering over the Berlin Wall into communist East Germany. I felt like I was at a zoo, spying on caged humans, their surroundings drab and grey. Freedom, individuality, and human rights, things I took for granted, were considered enemies of the state in that closed-in society. For several young Americans during the early Vietnam era, the concept of assisting others threatened by communism was almost instinctual.

Andy had somehow found a letter from 1970 written to Mount Pleasant's local newspaper by Glenn's parents after their son's death. He e-mailed it to me to share with the others. The letter was in response to an earlier editorial criticizing soldiers involved in the Vietnam conflict. The following is a part of that letter:

"Before our son departed for Vietnam, we talked at great length on our involvement there and his feelings about going. He talked about the French helping us gain our independence and said now these people (South Vietnamese) need our help in the same manner." Glenn's parents went on to write: *"Glenn Jr. left here not with malice or hatred for the North Vietnamese but with the firm conviction that all mankind should have the right to choose his or her form of government...."*

The four of us sat with our coffees and silently contemplated Glenn's sense of duty and his parents' anguish. I again reflected on what a remarkable group of guys we were honoring.

The day was even hotter than the previous one, already ninety degrees by 9 am, predicted to exceed one-hundred degrees by noon. The air was heavy, and the first fifteen to twenty miles of to-day's ride were on a busy four-lane highway with a thin shoulder. Despite the weather and riding conditions, Dave had renewed energy, almost completely recovered from bothersome chafing he had endured over the previous few days.

I drove the car the first shift and merged onto a four-lane road toward Chesapeake Bay. Traffic was heavy, bumper-to-bumper in spots. After twelve miles, I found an unpaved turn off with a flat area I could pull the Subaru into. I waited for the others, and they crested a hill into my line of vision about ten minutes later. They saw me and veered off the road toward the car, walking their bikes across a rough dirt road to where I was parked. Stephanie was frustrated with the traffic and worried about Dave. Riding this stretch was not enjoyable, but we felt compelled to continue. Stephanie agreed to drive the car, but only after I reassured her that I would stay behind Dave and keep him as far off the road as possible.

We set off again through undeveloped land broken up by frequent commercial intersections. The traffic did not abate, and drivers were impatient and unforgiving. Some yelled obscenities and seemed to intentionally crowd us off the road. I became increasingly incensed at the rudeness of the masses whizzing by; I wanted to put a big sign on Dave's bike: *"Show a little respect. Disabled Vietnam veteran honoring fallen comrades."* But my rational side realized nobody really gave a shit. Except us. Those passing us were too busy with their mundane, hurried lives.

After switching car drivers a few times, we made our way to Route 50, the road which crossed the Chesapeake Bay. It was a major highway, but at least sported a wide shoulder. As we neared the Bay, we exited the highway and navigated lesser traveled roads that continued over a narrow peninsula connected by short bridges to islands extending toward the long bridge we would have to cross by car. Our spirits soared as we smelled the brackish water and caught occasional glimpses of the Chesapeake. We found a bike path that paralleled the road and hopped onto it, glad to escape traffic noise and exhaust fumes. We stopped several times to take pictures with the Bay as our backdrop. I had never stood on its shores before.

The heat was so overwhelming that we needed to refill our water bottles every twenty to thirty minutes. After noon, we entered Stevensville, the "end of the road" for biking. We met up with Stephanie, who had driven the last leg, and found a pub to have lunch. Covering thirty miles had taken us four hours; we were hot, dirty, a little pissed off, and famished. When the four of us walked through the doors, the waitress informed us that the heat index outside was well over 120 degrees. Advisories on television recommended staying inside, and she chastised us for biking in such weather. We were too exhausted to explain our story and defend ourselves.

The morning's ride had broken our brash spirit. Each of us knew that traffic would only worsen once we crossed the Bay. We couldn't locate any biking routes on Google Maps from Annapolis leading through the suburbs into downtown Washington. After much discussion, we agreed that unless we found a road with a safe, wide shoulder, we would drive thirty miles to the outskirts of Washington, check into a hotel, and then park our car on Saturday morning at Rock Creek State Park and take the Rock Creek Bike Path the fifteen or so miles into central D.C. We felt like we were selling out, at least to some degree, but hey, safety is safety. The four of us had travelled so far, and we were determined to get Dave to the Wall. We'd been fortunate since leaving Plum Beach with no real incidents, and we didn't want to make a foolish decision just to keep bikes (and Dave) on the road.

It was luxurious lingering in the cool, dry air conditioning after spending the morning in unrelenting heat and humidity. We felt no pressure to head outside and resume our travels. After lunch, we sat quietly, each sipping a beer. We were mentally drained. I thought back on what we had accomplished over the preceding days and wondered what the next two days would bring.

Dave broke the silence. With a determined look on his face, he stated, "I'm gonna contact Roger Bergh."

I responded, "The Lieutenant in the Command and Control helicopter?"

Dave nodded, "Yes. I owe it to you guys to find out the details of that morning. I should have contacted Roger long ago. I think I have held out all these years because I was angry…or scared. But now I…no, WE need to know."

The three of us looked at Dave and reassured him that he didn't owe us anything. In fact, we owed him—for letting us be part of his story, for introducing us to a group of young heroes, and for leading us on such a memorable trip.

Stephanie said, "Dave, you can contact Roger, and we will support you. But please don't think you owe us anything."

Dave replied, "It's the right thing to do, long overdue. I found his Facebook contact earlier this morning and messaged him. Hopefully, he'll respond."

The four of us sat silently, collectively wondering if Roger Bergh would answer and if so, what the consequences would be. We were entering uncharted territory.

We finished lunch and exited to the parking lot. It felt like a sauna outside. After loading the bikes on the car and merging onto the highway, we crossed Chesapeake Bay and made our way through Annapolis. There were no roadways with shoulders that allowed for safe biking, and there was no letup in traffic. Feeling defeated we decided to end the day's ride. We found a hotel just off the beltway, about five miles from the northern aspect of the bike path we planned to take into the heart of Washington the following morning.

After checking into our rooms, I caught up on e-mails and then decided to go for a swim in the hotel pool. As I passed through the lobby, I ran into Dave, Stephanie, and Coleman. They were relaxing in easy chairs, engaged in what looked like serious conversation. When I walked over to them, Dave looked up. "I heard from Roger Bergh. He's calling at 8 am tomorrow."

I sat down in the chair next to Dave. "So, you're taking the call?"

Dave smiled. "No…WE are taking the call. I'm gonna put him on speaker phone. Eight am in Steph's and my room. I want you guys to hear it firsthand, and you are welcome to ask him questions. We are a team!"

Dave still had no knowledge of the crowd coming to greet him in D.C. I'd been talking with Andy throughout the afternoon, trying to coordinate the surprise. Andy and I decided that when the four of us were about sixty minutes away from the Wall, I would text Andy so he could position the others. After Dave, Steph, Coleman, and I found Joy on the National Mall, the welcoming crowd would casually walk out of the shadows and surround Dave at our meeting spot. I was certain that Dave would appreciate and possibly need the support of our expanded circle of friends as we then paid our respects at the Wall.

As I sat in bed that night, I posted a summary on Facebook.

Facebook Post (Jim) Friday, September 9, 2016

… One final thought or thoughts. I'm not sure why I proposed the idea of this week's crazy adventure to Dave. I'm also not sure how it ended up being the four of us. To be honest, once we decided we would do it, I didn't really give the trip much thought. I was busy with other things, and the trip took on a life of its own, a comical prospect to many of our friends. "You are doing what? Do you even own a bike?" As I finish the week, I'm pretty sure that what

motivated me was the fact that I was extremely fortunate to have missed this war. I'm sure Dave has survivor's guilt. "Why me? Why did I survive?" I think those who are my age look at Dave and feel a little guilty too. "Why him...and them...all those brave young men?" What Steph, Coleman, and I really want Dave to know is that we have his back. That if we were in that situation, without hesitation, we too would have flown into that hell and done our best to pull him out of there...

I finished writing around midnight, but I was too filled with nervous anticipation to fall asleep. I tossed and turned and then sat up and opened my iPad. I realized I knew very little about the Vietnam War even though I had lived through it as a kid and was now rehashing it on a daily basis. I very clearly remembered images and film clips from childhood–Richard Nixon, Hueys, soldiers' faces, bombs exploding in the jungle, flag-draped coffins. But even now, I didn't really understand the war. I spent the next two hours reading about Vietnam.

Ostensibly, our involvement started as an effort to thwart the spread of Communism. Vietnam was already split in two, with the North ruled by a communist regime aligned with Russia and China. At the height of the Cold War, as a nation, we were deeply threatened by the Domino Theory—the presumption that if one Southeast Asian country fell to communism, others, in short order, would follow. We had witnessed this phenomenon in Eastern Europe after World War II.

Our initial intent was to assist South Vietnam in ousting North Vietnamese communist sympathizers, the Viet Cong. With time, we mostly achieved that goal, but at the cost of a growing number of young American lives. As the North Vietnamese Army (NVA) supported by Russia and China became increasingly involved, the conflict escalated. In technical terms we were winning the war on the ground. We clearly had supreme military might. But politically, the American public was divided, and as the body count continued to increase, the political will to support an expanding conflict waned. Ho Chi Minh, the president of North Vietnam, had predicted this. Years earlier, he had proclaimed: "You will kill ten of our men, and we will kill one of yours, and in the end, it will be you who tire of it."

By the summer of 1970, our leaders in Washington had approved initiating the process of "Vietnamization," turning the responsibility for fighting the war over to South Vietnam's Army of the Republic of Vietnam (ARVN). The U. S. Senate had determined that this war was not worth its price. Over the following two years, the focus shifted from a further build up to figuring out how to respectfully end our involvement and withdraw without leaving our ally, the South Vietnamese, completely high and dry.

Given the terrain, jungle environment, and nature of fighting, Army Infantry activated Ranger units in Vietnam in 1969. Rangers had operated during World War II and the Korean War as long-range reconnaissance patrols, working behind enemy lines. In Vietnam, the goal was to "out-guerilla" the guerillas.

Service as a Ranger was voluntary. A soldier needed to be airborne qualified and willing and able to take on and master advanced training in all aspects of ground combat—weaponry, close contact fighting, radio communications, map reading, and medical. Dave's fight was mostly against the NVA. The base he worked out of was just south of the DMZ. It was surrounded by Viet Cong and the NVA. NVA soldiers were well trained, heavily armed, and especially adept at jungle warfare.

Ranger teams consisted of six soldiers, sometimes with scouts, and their job was to infiltrate behind enemy lines and disrupt the opposition by gathering information, planting explosives, taking prisoners, and setting up ambushes. Teams carried everything they needed, and their missions were usually completed over five days with extraction at a prearranged site by helicopter. They were greatly outnumbered, far from reinforcements, and it was not unusual for a small team of Rangers to be overrun by an entire company of NVA soldiers. At such times, Rangers would be forced to fight against staggering odds.

The Army Rangers in Vietnam lived by one overriding rule: do whatever you have to do to survive. There were no illusions about the nobility of their mission when in the bush. They battled against a fierce, determined enemy, and because of their circumstances, they existed as a brotherhood. They fought for themselves and for each other. Aside from the daring helicopter pilots and crewmen, there were probably no other soldiers who consistently assumed greater risk.

As I pictured Dave's elite fighting force on the ground slogging through the jungle of Vietnam, I couldn't help but think to myself how confusing the outcome of a war is and what "winning" or "losing" a war really means. In terms of Vietnam, it is widely accepted that the United States lost the war. Technically, this might be correct, but in no way does that "loss" reflect upon the soldiers who fought it.

After staring at images from long ago on my iPad, my mind turned to the present. My daughter Meg had recently toured Vietnam during a vacation from teaching in Thailand. Same land. Same climatic conditions. Same pinpointed location on earth. I wondered if Meg crossed any of the ground that Dave had walked over 46 years earlier. The thought brought me back to when I had walked the grounds of Andersonville and realized I was retracing JKP Ferrell's footsteps. Once again, I came to the startling realization that we all walk the same soil. The geography doesn't change. The only change is the passage of time.

CHAPTER 22
Connecting with Roger and Riding for Dale

Day 7 (Saturday, September 10, 2016)

I awoke early with mixed emotions—excitement about the day ahead; relief that we had almost reached our goal; gratitude that we were safe and in one piece; a tinge of sadness that we were nearing the end of our adventure. I realized it was my brother Joe's birthday. I texted him and told him where I was and what I was doing. I referred him to my Facebook posts, all of which he read in one sitting. He responded, "Bro, you are the man!"

The four of us met for an early breakfast and then assembled in Steph and Dave's room at 7:50 am. As I sat staring at the phone with the other three, I wondered what was going through Dave's head. Was he anxious about the upcoming call and the details it might render, the pain it might cause? Was he excited about reconnecting and putting things to rest? I couldn't help but feel some angst, again questioning whether I (we) had pushed Dave too hard on this journey into the past. But Dave's desire to reconnect with Bergh made me think that going back was the only way for him to reconcile and break free from the tragedy he could not erase. It had happened. He had been a part of it. Eleven precious lives had been lost. The facts would never change. It was not his fault, and he needed to move forward.

Steph, obviously harboring similar reservations, broke the silence. "Dave, no matter what we learn, you are a great husband, father, and friend."

Coleman and I nodded our heads in agreement. Coleman added, "We are here for you brother. We are a team."

Dave smiled. "I'm okay with this. It's time to close the loop."

At precisely 8 am, the phone rang, and Dave answered, putting it on speaker. The next hour was one of the most intense, interesting, emotional hours of my life. Roger gave us a detailed account, everything he remembered about that fateful morning 46 years ago.

As described in *The Price of Exit*, Dave's Huey was just off the ground, roaring in at full speed when it suddenly did a forward 360 resulting in immediate impact and explosion. Upon witnessing the crash, the command and control Huey initiated a corkscrew landing into the DMZ and settled near the downed Ranger chopper. Lieutenant Bergh and the other commanding officer, Captain Fred Johnson, jumped out and ran toward the burning helicopter. In the smoky haze, like an apparition, Dave walked out of a flaming, oil slickened, water-filled bomb crater. The downed Huey was nearby, throwing off intense heat and thick suffocating smoke, which made it difficult to get too close. The water had softened Dave's landing and saved his life. He was badly shaken and disoriented, but without major injuries.

Bergh loaded Dave onto the command helicopter, waved it off, and stayed on the ground with Johnson. The two officers searched for survivors as sniper fire hit around them. Shortly thereafter, as the NVA began bracketing mortar rounds into the crash site, forward soldiers from the rifle platoon arrived on scene. Between the burning chopper, small arms fire, and the mortar barrage, chaos reigned. The third mortar round killed Richard Stube and Michael Linville. They were crouched within yards of Bergh and Johnson, shooting back at snipers hidden in the trees. As the enemy fired the killing mortar into the crash site, the two officers found just enough cover behind a small rock, and though badly injured, both survived. Eventually, other assault helicopters and the infantry company beat back the North Vietnamese and secured the site.

The radio chatter that morning was nonstop. Ranger and helicopter teams throughout the region listened intently, feeling helpless, hoping and praying that some of their brothers had made it out. With time, most became aware of the lone survivor, Dave.

Roger checked in on Dave as both healed from their injuries in a combat hospital. Dave was almost catatonic, emotionally shellshocked, unable to remember anything about the event for days. Roger said there were discussions about inserting Dave back into active combat. Some thought he might recover from the psychologic trauma more quickly if forced into survivor mode. The doctors caring for Dave argued that he wasn't ready. They felt that placement back on the front lines could be devastating. It was determined that a non-combat job would be more appropriate until Dave's tour officially ended.

At the end of Bergh's narrative, there was a brief silence. Dave then apologized to Roger for never reaching out to him. He thanked Roger for saving his life. Through the phone line, it was easy to tell that Roger was genuinely happy, actually thrilled that Dave had recovered completely, gone on to lead a full life; that he had a good support system including a great wife and friends who were willing to go to bat for him. Steph, Coleman, and I asked questions to clarify certain details. Roger treated us with respect as if we were valued members of his team.

When the conversation ended, we said our goodbyes, all of us—including Roger—near or in tears. For five minutes, the four of us sat staring at the phone. And then we looked up at each other. A smile slowly formed on Dave's face as he stated, "Let's finish this mission."

We organized our gear and loaded our bikes onto the car. We drove fifteen minutes to Rock Creek State Park, silently reflecting on the morning's phone call. I felt conflicted about finishing our journey and overwhelmed by the prospect of visiting the Wall— over 58,000 names, among them eleven young men who we felt were our guys. We had looked at their pictures, read their bios, and ridden with them all week. We were ready to honor them at THEIR memorial.

We were right on schedule to meet Joy at the Wall around 11 am. She had flown into D.C. earlier that morning, and I had already spoken with her and planned our rendezvous. Others in the welcoming contingent had been arriving since Thursday, and everyone was lodging downtown, just off the National Mall.

After parking the car, the four of us walked our bikes to the start of the bike path. We stood there solemnly staring at each other. Dave reminded us that we were riding for his fifth Ranger teammate, Dale Allen Gray, a 20-year-old from Mesa, Arizona. Dale was trained as a medic, referred to as "Doc" by many of the soldiers at Base Camp. He had completed several missions and attended to multiple wounded warriors. Dale was especially admired for his "bedside" manner, and this fit with Dave's description—a team oriented, unselfish spirit. I couldn't help but notice the sadness in Dave's eyes as he described yet another exceptional young man.

After Dave finished speaking, we stood in a small circle, quietly staring at our feet. I looked up at the other three and said, "This morning, our final day, we ride for Dale. Dale was a healer, and as we finish our ride, I feel his presence. I sense that he hopes this trip has brought Dave some inner peace and acceptance." I paused and then continued, "Dave, thank you. It has been an honor and a privilege to be a part of your team, with the spirits of your, and now our, eleven brothers."

Dave, Steph, Coleman, and I collectively appreciated our good fortune at sharing these final few minutes of the ride together. A part of me wanted to grab the hands of the clock and slow down time. I wished to stay in the moment and extend the bond forged with my co-riders. The four of us had supported one another for 400-plus miles over six days. We had connected with eleven young men who had died tragically 46 years ago. Though I wasn't quite ready to cross the finish line of this trip, there was nothing standing in our way. It was time to bring it home.

As we started pedaling, I lingered in the rear. I called Andy to let him know where we were and our anticipated time of arrival. I told him that Joy would be meeting us at the end of the Wall closest to the Washington Monument and asked him to have the rest of the group assembled nearby.

The Rock Creek bike path started out as a wide road, and we were initially able to ride side by side. As we got closer to downtown, the trail became more crowded with blind corners, sharp curves, steep inclines, and two-way traffic. We rode carefully, single file, hesitant to push it hard and risk injury when so close to our destination. As we came upon the Potomac River, the path widened and visibility improved. We passed the Watergate Hotel and the Kennedy Center for the Performing Arts on our left and shortly thereafter came up to the rear of the Lincoln Memorial. We crossed the road, veered onto a sidewalk, coasted right past the group of Plum Beachers hidden among the trees, and caught sight of the Wall. We dismounted from our bikes and slowly pushed them toward our destination. The Wall, shining in the late morning's hazy sun, was already crowded with visitors.

We leaned our bikes against a fence and walked toward Joy who was jumping up and down and waving wildly at us. We caught up with her, and each of us gave her a hug. The five of us huddled together just off the end of the Wall. And then neighbors and friends started streaming in. Dave's face lit up with surprise. And then jubilation. And then raw emotion as 26 people lined up and each embraced him. I watched the procession of people, our support team, many with tears in their eyes, all there to honor Dave and the memory of eleven young men who had perished in the jungle. I looked at Dave, tears streaming down his face. It was a wonderful sight, tender and uplifting—a testament to friendship and the goodness in people.

September 10, 2016 was another sweltering day, but we barely noticed as our large group moved in unison toward and then along the Wall. We found the eleven names, etched in granite next to each other. Eleven guys brought together that morning 46 years ago under circumstances beyond their control. As I stood staring at their names, a multitude of emotions swept over me. Sadness. Pride. Gratitude. Back to sadness. I thought of their families and friends. I considered the craziness of life, the randomness and unfairness. I wondered how Dave had walked away from that morning, and I again marveled at his inner strength. I hoped our ride had brought him reconciliation and comfort.

That evening we held a ceremony to celebrate Dave and honor the soldiers who died the morning of September 20, 1970. Andy acted as emcee, and several members of our group spoke. We toasted one another, laughed, and shed tears together, thirty living souls feeling the spirits of the eleven young soldiers in our midst. It was the perfect finale to an incredible journey.

CHAPTER 23
Moving On

Later that evening, Joy and I returned to our hotel room. Joy was exhausted and immediately fell asleep. Unable to sleep, I rolled out of bed, crept out of our room, and wandered up to the rooftop bar of our hotel, still open with a few late-night stragglers quietly conversing in small groups. I sat alone at a corner table and looked out over the city. The Washington Monument was lit up; the White House little more than a stone's throw away. It was after midnight and still very warm—a beautiful summer night.

As I sipped a cold glass of wine, I thought about the previous week. I was overwhelmed with emotions, still recovering from the endorphin rush that resulted from the day's events. I pictured my Joy, soundly asleep in our room below and my two daughters, Meg braving a year in Thailand and Kate adjusting to college and her newfound independence. I contemplated the bike journey just completed, something I would never be able to replicate, and the bond forged between

Steph, Dave, Coleman, and me: the four "road warriors." I knew I would never forget the eleven real warriors who had made the ultimate sacrifice that morning in the jungle. They were now a part of me. It was an added bonus sharing the experience with so many, not just those in D.C., but also extended family members, close friends back home, and multiple others who followed and supported us on Facebook. For one week, it felt like we had created a buzz, our own little community.

Coleman posted his reflections on Facebook before he went to sleep.

Facebook Post (Coleman) Saturday evening, September 10, 2016

Honor and privilege are two terms that come to mind when I think of this fantastic trip. I am honored to have been a part of such a wonderful adventure! I am privileged to have been born in America. Biking the east coast was inspirational. I do not say this lightly! I am fortunate to have such outstanding friends as Dave, Jimmy, and Steph. Love and thanks for all the support from family and friends.

The next morning, Joy caught a ride to the airport with some of our Plum Beach friends. Coleman and his wife, Linda, who had flown in the day before to be part of the welcoming delegation, flew back to Florida. Stephanie, Dave, and I loaded our bikes onto Joy's Subaru one last time and drove back to Rhode Island. The prospect of returning to work and other aspects of our routine existences seemed daunting, as if it might take a period of readjustment to become a "civilian" again. We drove into Plum Beach around 8 pm Sunday night, and the next day we jumped back into our normal lives.

Facebook Post (Dave) Monday, September 12, 2016

Well, this is my final post. Saturday was an incredible day, one of the most rewarding, emotional, and powerful days of my life. I had

*found former Lt. Roger Bergh on Facebook the day before and ar-
ranged to have a phone conversation with him on Saturday morning.
I had gone 46 years, unable to make that call, and he, likewise. I
don't know why, and it doesn't really matter. Left to my own devices,
I might never have made that call. But I felt I owed it to my cycling
partners to address this final piece of the puzzle. This is their story
too. I invited Steph, Jim, and Cole to take part in my call.*

*We waited anxiously for the phone to ring. At 8 am sharp, he
called, and for the next hour, in vivid detail, Roger described the
events of that morning. Our conversation ended and we four sat in
my hotel room, stunned by the revelations. We then made our way
into D.C. on our bikes, I thought to meet Jim's wife, Joy, who had
flown in from RI. As we pulled up to the Wall, friends, and neighbors
from Plum Beach enveloped us. We gathered at the Wall, hugged,
and wept. Later, we held a ceremony at our Hotel, honoring those
who died September 20, 1970.*

CHAPTER 24
The Aftermath of the Bike Ride

Unbeknownst to me, our journey had so captivated my daughter Meg that she contacted *The Providence Journal*, Rhode Island's daily newspaper. Meg thought Dave's story and our ride were worthy of more widespread attention and needed to be shared with the greater Rhode Island community. She communicated by e-mail from Thailand with one of the newspaper's feature writers, and the weekend after we returned home, that journalist and a photographer came to Plum Beach to interview us and take pictures. On September 21, 2016 our ride was featured on the front page of the *"ProJo"* with pictures and a detailed summary. Entitled "Riding with Honor," the piece accurately depicted the back story and recognized Dave and the soldiers involved.

Two days after arriving back in Rhode Island, I wrote my final Facebook post. I sat in bed and reflected over the previous week's journey and the day in D.C. and considered the back story.

For over an hour, I felt paralyzed by emotion, unable to write. I was unsure where to start or what my message should be. And then I pictured Bergh's helicopter diving into the active war scene and the two young infantrymen racing forward to help the downed chopper. As I stated in an earlier Facebook post, I'd like to think that had I been in their positions, I would have done the same. Heroes come in all shapes and forms, and most heroic actions are not planned. They are instinctive, situational. I think humans are innately good and that every one of us has heroic potential. Thankfully, most of us are not placed in situations where we need to prove it. Those brave men were, and some paid with their lives.

I found my words and wrote the following ending summation:

Final Facebook Post (Jim) Tuesday evening, September 13, 2016.

After much thoughtful consideration, Dave decided he would try to contact Roger Bergh, the Army Lieutenant who was in the command helicopter coordinating the insertion of Dave's team. On the 6th day of the ride, Dave messaged him on Facebook, heard back shortly thereafter, and we coordinated a phone call for 8 am the following day. The four of us listened in by speaker phone. It was very emotional for Dave, but we were able to corroborate several details of that fateful morning and fill in some missing information. The phone call lasted for about an hour.

The command helicopter was above the Huey carrying Dave's Ranger team, giving orders, directing the insertion site, and maintaining close radio contact. Dave's helicopter was flying just below the treetops at over 100 mph heading to the agreed upon insertion site. Roger told us he will never forget the visual of Dave's helicopter crash. The Ranger Huey was flying straight in when it suddenly did a quick, complete, 360 degree somersault in the air and barreled into a bomb crater in the DMZ. Upon impact, it exploded and caught fire. Dave was thrown from the helicopter when or before it crashed into the bomb crater, landing in oil slickened, burning water.

When the command helicopter saw Dave's Huey go down, the pilot immediately banked and made the most perfectly executed corkscrew landing into the site of the crash. At about the same time, members of a forward infantry team already on the ground heard and/or saw the crash and rushed to the scene. There was sniper fire coming in from North Vietnamese soldiers nearby. Roger and his commanding officer, Captain Fred Johnson, set off to search for survivors while the forward infantry soldiers set up a perimeter around the crash site.

Upon landing, the Lieutenant found Dave walking out of the bomb crater, conscious and bleeding but without apparent life-threatening injuries. Dave was placed in the command helicopter while the two officers stayed on the ground and searched for other survivors. The downed helicopter was burning badly, and Lieutenant Roger got as close to it as possible. The wreckage was mostly unidentifiable molten debris.

The terrain around the crash site was half open and half elephant grass. Two members of the infantry team took positions on their knees looking out for and firing back at snipers hidden in the surrounding brush. Roger and Captain Johnson were right next to those two Army soldiers when mortar rounds started coming in. The Lieutenant and Captain hit the ground, and Roger found a stone to get his head behind. The third round of mortars instantly killed the two kneeling soldiers, and both officers took multiple shrapnel hits. Luckily Roger's head was behind the rock and the Captain was shielded by Roger, so though 39 pieces of shrapnel struck Roger, his head was spared.

The crew medevacked Dave out in the command and control helicopter. I am not sure how Bergh and Johnson were evacuated, but both returned to action after recovering from their injuries, survived the war, and went on to have distinguished careers after Vietnam. Now retired, Lieutenant-Colonel Roger Bergh has a slight southern drawl and speaks in a very thoughtful and deliberate manner. One can tell by listening to him, that this is a caring, generous person, a good man, delighted after all these years to know that Dave ended up having a distinguished career, a rewarding life, and that he is loved by many.

Eleven men died that morning, all within a very short timeframe, nine in the helicopter and two securing the crash site as mortars rained. I would ask anyone reading this to say their names aloud, let them know they are not forgotten, and then say a prayer for their families and loved ones.

There is some question as to the cause of the helicopter crash. The pilot, First Lieutenant Albert Maurice Finn, a 26-year-old from Lansdale, Pennsylvania was described by Roger as meticulously attentive to detail, a gifted, experienced pilot, who had flown several Ranger insertions. It seems very unlikely that it was pilot error or mechanical failure that was causal. The helicopter was under heavy fire from the ground, and the leading speculation is that the enemy shot out the rear rotor blade. This would make the helicopter impossible to maneuver and account for its abrupt 360-degree spiral before crashing. The other men in the helicopter died instantly. How Dave walked out of that crater is nothing short of miraculous.

I am not sure if the officers gave an order to descend or if the pilot responded instinctively, but had they not gone in, Dave probably would have been killed by sniper fire or mortar rounds. Dave, of course, does not remember any of this.

We learned all this on the last day of our ride. When we reached the Wall, several of Dave's closest friends were there to meet us. This was a surprise to Dave. More emotion on top of a very poignant morning which was the end of a very inspirational week. I think the pictures that we posted tell that part of the story better than

I can in writing, so I'm not going to describe the scene of all those people there to support Dave or the celebration we had the rest of that day well into the evening. I think my friend Ed said it best later that night, something along the lines of, "It's not that Dave survived Vietnam that's so remarkable, it's the way he's lived his life after Vietnam that is an inspiration to all of us."

Now that the journey is over, I mostly have memories of great scenery, shared experience, friendship, laughter, and becoming one with my bike. I feel like I got to know a little bit about eleven young guys who fought a war that was a "little backward" (to quote an unnamed but very legitimate source), courageous guys who died way too young. I also feel like I better understand what Dave went through, and I am more amazed that somehow, he got past the bloodshed and dying, grabbed life, ran with it, and continues to do so.

For several weeks after completing the ride, I contemplated all the ways it had impacted me. After living and breathing the fateful events in Vietnam, I had difficulty pulling away and regrouping. The spirits of the men who perished that morning had propelled us over 400 miles. I missed being out on the road with them. I missed my teammates. I frequently visited the Ranger Team 1-8 Facebook page and repeatedly watched a YouTube video that Dave made called *7W Army Rangers*. I also found myself revisiting the motorhome trip I had taken twelve years earlier and re-experiencing the special bond that trip had forged between my family members and JKP Ferrell, a long forgotten Civil War soldier. The two trips were so different yet felt so similar.

One of my Facebook friends, Jeff Redinger, someone I haven't seen since middle school, followed our ride closely. He was incredibly supportive every step of the way. He understood the difficulties one might encounter following such an experience. After my last Facebook post, he commented:

"How does one go back to work after an adventure like that? New scenery, new acquaintances, personal stories, and a big purpose and goal to work toward...Thanks for taking me/us along and sharing this uplifting story..."

With time, I eventually digested the experience and accepted it for what it was—a once in a lifetime, unexpected, intensely rewarding odyssey. Like all journeys, it had to end. But it inspired me to share it with others, to put it into words. And it has instilled in me a quiet confidence, a will to challenge myself, break through barriers and defy limitations, imposed by others and even placed on me by myself.

When I began writing this narrative, I didn't know that the story would continue to evolve, but it did. In August 2017, Roger Bergh and his wife, Carol, visited Plum Beach, and Joy and I had the privilege of hosting a dinner party in their honor. Most of the Washington contingent attended, Andy again acting as emcee. In June 2018, after decades of avoiding the ghosts of his past, Dave hosted a Vietnam Army Ranger reunion at our neighborhood beach club. Fred Johnson, the Captain in the command and control helicopter, was a special guest. My neighbors and I have thus had the opportunity to meet other Vietnam Army Rangers who served with Dave in addition to both of his superior officers, to recognize their actions and personally thank them. Both experiences were memorable extensions of the bike ride story. Both brought us to tears (again). And both brought added (though probably never complete) closure for Dave.

When we hosted the dinner party for Roger Bergh and his wife Carol the summer following our bike trip, Roger shared details about his career in the army which ended shortly after being part of the liberating force in Kuwait during the first Gulf War. He was one of the first American Army officers to enter Kuwait City after

American forces drove the Iraqis out. When he rode into the city, the local citizens poured out of their homes and rushed to him to offer their gratitude. Everywhere he went, people hugged him, invited him into their homes, and offered him gifts. For several days, he was the guest of honor of an entire city. When Roger came back from Vietnam, nobody expressed appreciation or acknowledged his service. Our dinner party was the first time he EVER received a formal, personal thank you for his service in Vietnam. He told us this sad fact with tears in his eyes.

Earlier, on the day the Berghs visited our neighborhood, my then 19-year-old daughter Kate expressed a desire to meet Roger and Carol. Roger was arriving into the neighborhood at approximately 4 pm, and Kate needed to be in Massachusetts for a dinner with her future college roommates by 5 pm. As the afternoon progressed, I told Kate she was cutting it too close; that Roger might be late, delaying her departure and the meeting with her friends. She turned to me with a surprised look in her eyes and said, "Dad, this guy saved Dave's life. I can't imagine what my life would be like without Dave and Stephanie in it. I want to meet this guy and thank him. My friends can wait."

The Berghs arrived at the Slone's around 4:30 pm, and after they settled, Kate and I went up to see them. We made small talk for five to ten minutes and then Kate gave Roger and Carol a hug and we left, Kate off to Boston and me home to prepare for the evening's dinner party. At the end of the evening, Roger came up to me, and he thanked me for bringing Kate up to meet him and Carol earlier that day. He said something along the lines of, "I can't believe a young person would want to meet and honor an old guy like me." Yet, another example of the impact he had on our lives and the generation following us, totally unknown to him.

Roger Bergh told us one story at our dinner party that I must include. It emphasizes the random nature of destiny or perhaps the occasional offered hand of divine provenance. In this case, I think more likely the latter, as Roger's future wife Carol was praying especially hard for Roger the morning of Dave's helicopter crash.

When the North Vietnamese fired mortars into the crash site, they used a technique known as bracketing, shooting a long and then a short to enable them to zero in on the exact target. As Roger and Fred were searching for survivors, Roger heard and saw the first two mortars come in, one going long, the second going short. He knew the third was likely to hit, and when he heard it fired, he hit the ground with Fred next to him. He yelled at the soldiers kneeling next to him to do the same, but they maintained their positions firing back at NVA snipers hidden amongst the trees. There was a small rock protruding out of the mud, and Roger chose to get his head to the right side of the rock. In the second or so that he waited for the third mortar to hit, he thought back to his high school football playing days. As captain of the team his senior year, he often had to call the coin toss at the start of games. He got every call wrong! In fact, as he laid stretched out on the ground, he couldn't recall ever getting a heads/tail call correct. He'd chosen to get to the right side of the rock. Should he have gone left? Right or left? Heads or tails? Too late to change his decision; he was due for a correct call. These thoughts were all going through his head. Thankfully, Roger chose the right (and correct) side of that rock.

I will never forget the end of that evening. It was a typical clear and comfortable New England August night, a slight breeze blowing through our porch. Most of our guests had departed, and I strolled into the kitchen and found Roger and Dave engaged in quiet conversation. They then embraced. Roger's wife, Carol, came up behind me and softly commented, "Those two are the legacy of so many fine young men, now mostly forgotten." I considered her words and realized what a tremendous burden the two humble giants in front of me bore. I again experienced immense gratitude that I had been invited in and allowed to be a small part of their story.

The Bike Ride to the Wall

Dave, Steph, Coleman, and JZ in southern RI

JZ climbing out of the NYC subway

Visiting the Boss's turf

Lunch on the Jersey Shore

Riding the boardwalk

Closing in

Our supporters at the Wall

Dave's Ranger Team

(clockwise from bottom left): Anthony Gallina, Dave, Dale Gray, Glenn Ritchie, Raymond Apellido, Harold Sides

Huey Team

Dan Felts

William Dotson

Larry Baldwin

Albert Finn

Infantry Members

Michael Linville

Richard Stube

ACKNOWLEDGEMENTS
(and a few clarifications)

I imagine my high school basketball experience sounds a bit like an exaggerated "Glory Days" tale (thanks again Bruce), but I think it was much more than that. I'd like to believe that my team was at least partly responsible for bridging the racial divide that existed at Deerfield Beach High School when I started there in 1972. We showed that as a mixed racial team, we were collectively much better than any of us as individuals. We had one great player, but the rest of us came together, with purpose and without ego. Jimmy Morgan, the most competitive athlete I have ever known, was gentle, quiet, and unassuming off the court. He was our leader. He led by example, playing the game of basketball with an intensity that made everyone around him better. Thankfully, his influence stayed with me off the court. I'm quite sure my life would have been harder had I not run into Jimmy that day in the gym. To this day, when I find myself faltering, in need of strength, I dig down and ask myself (hearing Jimmy's voice), "Z, you ready?"

In addition to Jimmy, I have to single out two other high school teammates. The first is George Bowls (AKA "Parrot"). George was a reserve forward. He was (and I'm sure still is) the nicest human being I have ever encountered. He was (is) kindness personified! When I find myself having a bad moment, I sometimes think of George. I picture his warm smile, and it always lifts my spirit and reassures me of the goodness in this world. Second, I have to expand on Al Beal who I described as "soft" in the first chapter of this book. Sorry Al! Let me clarify that after joining our team, Al became passionate about basketball and worked harder than any of us to improve his skills. He became stronger and emerged from high school as an elite player. He went on to play college basketball at Oklahoma University, leading the Sooners to the "Sweet 16" his junior year. He was subsequently drafted into the NBA but chose instead to play professional basketball in Europe. I could write an entire book containing Al stories; there is abundant material. But what is most amazing about Al is that despite all his success, underneath his serious and reserved demeanor, there is still a heart of gold. He never stops giving back—to his family, friends (near and far), and community. His actions and humility inspire all who know him, and I feel especially blessed to call him my friend.

John Knox Polk Ferrell was just a farm boy from Ohio, no different than thousands of others who heeded the call and volunteered to serve in the Grand Army of the Republic. He endured over seven months in one of the worst POW camps in the history of mankind. In remembrance of his imprisonment, he whittled a simple wooden mallet, and somehow that mallet survived intact for the next 100 plus years and found its way into my father's hands.

I periodically take out the mallet and examine it closely. When I hold it, I smile. I picture my father, Arlan, and me sitting together on a random evening fifteen years ago, before our motorhome trip, caressing the mallet and trying to figure out who this JKP character really was and what the mallet stood for. If JKP was looking down at us at that time, I have to believe our brainstorming session brought him great satisfaction and probably some humor. Three learned, successful, adult men, over a century later paying homage to his whittling skills. He surely never envisioned the journey his simple hand-made object would take us on or the connection it would forge between us and him. Or maybe he did. Either way, our lives are now, and forever, joined.

I sometimes wonder if JKP's living relatives have any awareness of his service in the Union Army, his stay at Andersonville, the life he led, or the mallet he carved. If not, it would be nice if they happened upon this story, learned that their ancestor not only served admirably but lived through great hardship with integrity and honor. And also, that he brought immense joy into my family members' lives. Sometimes we forget, but one of the weird things about life is that each one of us has the capacity to influence others every second of every day, sometimes immediately, sometimes remotely, sometimes directly, and sometimes indirectly; sometimes in ways we can't envision and will never know. When JKP carved that mallet, he had no idea of its long reaching consequences. He could not have foreseen that it would connect soldiers from three different wars over the span of 150-plus years. Through my father and now me, the mallet has done that.

After our motorhome trip, my father very much wanted to share JKP's saga and all its offshoots. I found ten pages of my dad's barely legible handwriting highlighting his struggle to find the best way to present JKP's story. As a historical novel? As a script for a movie or play? In the end, he concluded that just telling it like it happened, in narrative form, was the best way. That is what I have attempted to do.

I miss my dad. Writing this book has accentuated his, and now my mom's, absence. I hope my dad approves of the way I have constructed and told the Ferrell story. It's really his story. He put things into motion the day he walked out of that thrift shop with a 25-cent treasure. He chased down leads, crafted a tale, and invited me in. I was a fortunate observer. In regard to that chronic "disconnect" I experienced with my dad through an extended part of my earlier life, I feel we broke through and left it behind us for good on the motorhome trip. And I truly feel that the bike trip finally allowed me to play the "perfect game" my dad always expected out of me.

239

I also deeply miss Arlan, my brother-in-law. Arlan's illness and early death shattered my armor, ripped my heart out, and left me feeling raw, unsettled, and unsure. It destroyed my sister and three nephews. After his death, It took me several months to recover back to a semi-functional state, and I've never regained any semblance of the solid footing I thought I was planted on preceding his passage. Arlan was someone I looked forward to growing old with. He was a bright light, a beacon in my life. I always assumed his positivity and fun-loving nature would ease my journey; that we'd navigate the challenges of aging together and gracefully find our ways. What I miss most is his sense of humor and that snickering laugh.

My brother Joe is an amazing character—a blue collar, plain speaking genius. Desh raight, ah hah! You'd never realize it if you only superficially got to know him. However, if you dug below the surface, you would find immense, multidimensional talent. Joe could write a best-selling novel, build a spaceship, compose and play an elegant musical score, be a stand-up comic, and/or star in his own self-written comedy. My father often told me that if he was marooned on a remote deserted island and he had to choose one person to accompany him, he'd take Joe. A visual develops in my mind of the two of them washing ashore and within six months living in a mansion, lounging in hammocks, eating gourmet food. If they had Coleman with them, they could build an entire city from scratch.

I must thank Dave Slone for his friendship, guidance, and support. And even more, for sharing his story and joining me in telling it. Dave sets the bar high. Vietnam was a difficult war in so many ways. Like all wars, ordinary guys answered the call. Dave was one of them, too young at the time to understand completely what he was getting into. Unlike other wars, those who fought in Vietnam returned to a country torn apart. They were a casualty of the generational divide, largely unsupported and left to fend for themselves.

When you meet people like Dave, Roger, and other veterans who served in Vietnam, you realize there is no such thing as the "greatest generation." These guys sacrificed just as much, if not more than any other generation, under impossible circumstances. Most of them, like Dave, came back changed but found a way to carry on with their lives. Many of them did not return. **Harold Sides, Ray Apellido, Tony Gallina, Albert Finn, Larry Baldwin, Dan Felts, William Dotson, Richard Stube, Michael Linville, Glenn Ritchie, and Dale Gray** were eleven such guys who live on in the minds of my neighborhood friends and me through Dave. My friends and I know their faces and pray for their family members often.

For those of you who served in Vietnam and thankfully made it home, take heart knowing that most of your fellow countrymen now understand what you were asked to do and what you sacrificed. It certainly took longer than it should have, but I think I represent all present-day Americans in continuing the recognition and gratitude. Thank you!

I have several friends who were part of the anti-Vietnam war movement during the late sixties and early seventies. I am in no way diminishing the role they played in ending the war. If the populace, mostly young people, had not vigorously and sincerely opposed the war, it would have continued for much longer than it did. Sometimes we need to push our leaders to take the right action, in this case, to bring our soldiers home. Unfortunately, passion hindered clear thinking, and returning soldiers got caught in the middle, wrongly accused of being part of the problem, of being a part of "them." I hope our country learned a lesson from this and that it never happens again.

The motorhome and bike trips were two joyful experiences with great casts of characters, both trips with purpose. I'm not sure either journey would have gone so smoothly were it not for my travel companions. In addition to my dad, Arlan, Joe, and Dave, I will always feel indebted to my nephew David and to Stephanie and Coleman for being integral parts of such grand adventures, sharing their friendship and trust, and leaving me with such fantastic memories. Andy was also with us on the road, in spirit, every day during the bike trip to the Wall, so I also consider him one of my road-warrior mates. I also feel obliged to thank the Washington contingent and my Facebook friends from every phase of my life who were so involved and supportive during the bike trip. There are too many of you to name, but you know who you are!

Finally, Dr. David French, I promised you I would remind you of the conversation we had that afternoon on my porch preceding the bike trip. I thank you for the genuine concern you showed at the time (and the previous and subsequent wise guidance you have given me over the years). I will admit that you were right. The concept of the bike trip was a bit irrational; maybe even insane. But for some reason, my sane mind never interfered with my will to take on the mission. And my promise to you was ultimately fulfilled. I (we) got Dave to the Wall and home without a scratch.

Oh yes…home! I could only have planned and participated in both of the described spectacular trips with the encouragement and support of my family. So, I have to end with a shout out to my three "girls," Joy, Meg, and Kate. Thank you to my most special running mates. Thank you for being with me every step of the way. In the words of Neil Young (kind of), "long may WE run"…or maybe ride? The road is calling us…

EPILOGUE
September 7, 2019

The weather gods had blessed us again. Here we were, seven of us on bikes, stretched out like wings on either side of Dave, forming an arrow with Dave at its point as we prepared to cross the finish line of The New England Parkinson's Ride outside of Portland, Maine. Coleman was not present, but Steph, Dave, and I were joined by Joy, my sister Edie and nephew Jay from Colorado, and our friends Fred and David from our Plum Beach neighborhood. The rest of our team was waiting at the finish line. That morning, I had convinced Dave to ride thirty rather than the ten miles he had planned. I knew he doubted his ability to do the extra miles. He hadn't ridden much lately, and his Parkinson's had progressed since our bike trip three years previously. His positive, adventurous spirit, however, remained intact; he still loved a challenge. It only took a small amount of nudging. He knew I wasn't going to acquiesce, and after a few minutes, he looked up at me with that slow, crooked smile, and I knew I had him.

Hurricane Dorian was supposed to hit the region that morning, but at the last minute it had switched course, veered out to sea, and delivered in its wake a beautiful fall day. Now here we were, cruising to the endpoint, our leader flanked by his faithful legion of riders, Dave again proving that barriers were meant to be broken; with a little help from one's friends, anything was possible. Our supporters anxiously awaited our arrival. When we saw them, we raised our fists, and our boisterous fans jumped up and down. They rushed over to us as we crossed the finish line and found a spot away from the other participants. We got off our bikes and stood there, our small group of riders and friends, with arms raised and hands clasped together, silent, as if in prayer. I looked up at the blue sky and smiled with reverent appreciation.

My inner voice spoke, "Thank you:"

To my Dad for subtly imparting his wisdom and steadfastly supporting me;

To Arlan for always making me laugh;

To JKP Ferrell for taking five of us on a grand adventure and leaving my father with an indelible final chapter of life and me with a priceless keepsake;

And to Harold, Ray, Tony, Glenn, Dale, Albert, Larry, Dan, William, Michael, and Richard for teaching me the true meaning of courage and sacrifice.

Thanks guys! Thanks for pushing me onward. I wish you were here with me today, but you will always be in my heart.

ABOUT THE AUTHOR

James W. Ziegler (AKA Jim, Jimmy, JZ, Z) is a Pediatric Cardiologist at Hasbro Children's Hospital and an Associate Professor of Pediatrics at Brown University Medical School. His career has taken him from Florida to Boston to Colorado and then to Rhode Island where he has now lived for 25 years. He has been blessed with a very talented and supportive extended family and an extraordinary assortment of friends, neighbors, patients, and work colleagues. This book reflects a few of those unique interpersonal relationships and their unplanned consequences, what he likes to refer to as "human connectedness." James and his wife Joy, a pediatrician, live in Saunderstown, Rhode Island. They are the proud parents of two amazing young women, Meg and Kate.

Author's note: I took the liberty of changing a few individuals' names to protect their privacy.

-JWZ

Made in the USA
Middletown, DE
19 July 2021